CO-AQZ-500

"If your life is important to you, read this book, then give it to someone you love. Mr. Manko outlines simple steps that you can take today to protect yourself, your friends, and your family from the predatory threats lurking in our world. Best of all, he does this without instilling panic or fear in the reader, building on an underlying theme of humanity and compassion. Absolutely empowering."

KEVIN SECOURS, Director of Integrated Fighting Systems
and Author of *The Dragon Mind Method*

"Clearly the most practical, concise, informative, and eminently readable book on personal and family safety ever published. Ideal for everyone of every age level who wishes to realistically protect themselves and the lives of loved ones from the very real danger of violence in today's world. As a Family Law Attorney, I am very aware of the devastating results that violence can have in the lives of men, women, and children. This lifesaving book covers the broad range of violent acts, almost from birth to death, and offers the solutions to resolve, reduce, and prevent them. Get it before you or someone you love becomes a statistic."

ATTORNEY GREGG HERMAN, Vice Chair,
Family Law Section, American Bar Association

"Wesley Manko shares firsthand knowledge of wise self-defense practices to help keep us from threatening situations, and how to safely get out of them if we find ourselves confronted by them. Good basic self-defense tactics that work in the real-life situations any of us may confront at any time, providing the reader with a feeling of empowerment."

WENDY K. BAUMANN, President, The Wisconsin
Women's Business Initiative Corporation

"Practical self-defense information for adults and adolescents, especially for women and girls who care about their own personal safety."

MARY PLACKOWSKI, Outreach Services Director,
Advocates of Ozaukee, working to end domestic and sexual violence

"If you're serious about preventing violent crime, look no further than this book. These are real, proven self-defense strategies that can help you avoid violence and even save your life."
BOB FRISCH, President, Northshore Crime Stoppers, Milwaukee

"Wesley Manko's book is a good overview of practical ways to protect yourself and those you love. Whether you are caring for your children, thinking of your spouse or a single man or woman, this book helps you proactively think through a variety of situations. Based on years of research, experience, and training, Manko offers specific ways to deal with preventing harm and dealing with threatening situations. This book is a good resource guide for individual use or group study."
REV. SUSAN A. PATTERSON-SUMWALT, Senior Pastor of the United Methodist Church, Whitefish Bay, Wisconsin

"Insightful and informative advice for people of all ages and abilities. You don't have to be a martial artist to implement these practical lifesaving suggestions. The author offers an honest and realistic program that works by providing safe solutions to the many possibilities of violence that face each of us every day."
MASTER SAHNYA THOM, Tae Kwon Do Instructor and Owner of Alive and Kickin', Inc., Professional School of Martial Arts and Kickboxing

"This book has an immense amount of thought-provoking information as it relates to self-defense and everyday living. The author offers a unique and direct approach to a wide array of topics that could easily be an entire book series."
MASTER MARK GRIDLEY, Director/Founder of Anatomical Targeting Strategies

"Profoundly simple and insightful, Wes Manko's book effectively bridges the gap between sport martial arts and lethal military hand-to-hand combat techniques. This book will truly allow you to 'adapt to the fight' and is a must for anyone who desires to live with confident security. If you're an avid reader, make this book next on your list...if you're not, start here!"
MAJOR THOMAS GUALANDI, USMC

"Loaded with useful tips and great information."
CHRIS THOMAS, Coauthor of *Humane Pressure Point Self-Defense*

HOW TO
BE SAFE...
No Matter What

Wesley Manko, MPA

STRATEGIES FOR:
- ✓ Personal
- ✓ Family
- ✓ Workplace Self-Defense

BRONZE BOW PUBLISHING

How To Be Safe...No Matter What
Copyright © 2005 Wesley Manko

ISBN 1-932458-12-3

Published by Bronze Bow Publishing Inc.,
2600 E. 26th Street, Minneapolis, MN 55406

You can reach us on the Internet at www.bronzebowpublishing.com

Literary development and cover/interior design by
Koechel Peterson & Associates, Inc., Minneapolis, Minnesota.

Manufactured in the United States of America

To my wife
for helping my dreams
come true.

WESLEY MANKO is one of America's foremost personal safety and self-defense experts. His academic background includes college degrees in Police Science and Criminal Justice as well as a Master's Degree in Public Administration. His articles and views have been featured in a number of national publications, radio and television appearances. He has trained in numerous martial arts and is a Certified Systema Instructor. Some of his clients include women's domestic abuse prevention organizations, Fortune 500 companies, Girl Scouts, college students, as well as law enforcement and military personnel.

Table of Contents

Wherever a single name for a person has been used within this book, such as Linda or Pam, it is a fictional name that represents a composite of people's real-life experiences that I have summarized.

URGENT

Chapter
ONE

A Violent World

Violence Can Strike Anywhere

Chapter **ONE**
A Violent World

"The future depends on what we do in the present."
MAHATMA GANDHI

It was a day that began the same as any other day at the high school. Students scurried to class, teachers taught, and one boy would have his life changed.

The boy, who was emerging into manhood and fancied pursuing an acting career, walked inconspicuously down the hall to his next class. Then without warning, his left shoulder was struck from behind, causing him to spin around and drop his books.

"Hey!" the school bully shouted in the boy's face. "Why'd you hit me?"

Disorientated by the blow and confused, the young man didn't know what to say or how to respond. The school bully had hit him and not the vice versa. (Only much later would the boy learn that this is a common technique used by bullies of all ages.)

In about the time it takes to blink, the school bully grabbed the boy by his ankles and lifted him up. The boy felt his head smash into the concrete floor, and his glasses went flying in pieces from his face and scattered across the floor. The bully bounced the boy's head against the floor and taunted him in front of a gathered throng of students who stopped to watch the spectacle.

What seemed like an eternity of pain and torment was over in an instant. As the boy sat crumpled on the hallway floor, one of the bully's gang members handed him back his broken glasses. Spirit-crushing laughter echoed down the hallway, but faces were a mere blur.

A teacher's voice broke the revelry and ended the torment. "Boys, come with me." It was time to see the school principal.

As the boy trudged along behind the teacher, he anticipated the worst. But he was pleasantly shocked when the principal looked at him, smiled, and said, "Well, I think you learned your lesson." That was it. Somehow the reaction from the principal, who was also a Catholic priest, was more surprising than the scuffle.

When the boy went to his next class, the gym teacher asked, "Why didn't you kill the guy?" Clearly, the tyrant of the school hallways was despised by the faculty, and more than one teacher would be delighted to see the intimidator beaten. And back in the early 1970s what happened in a private school stayed in the private school.

This was a day that shattered many myths for the boy. For almost two years he had studied tae kwon do, and he could have even tested for a brown belt had he not quit to earn money a few months previous. What went wrong? He ran the attack scenario back over and over in his head. He realized that he had never been trained for this type of attack.

The next class began with another shock. One of the bully's gang members was in his class. The boy pretended not to notice him, but to no avail. He could neither run nor hide.

"Hey, where was your karate today?" the big creep jeered loudly.

Taunting laughter broke out in the classroom. Those who hadn't seen the short-lived fight had certainly heard about it from those who did. With a sickening feeling in his stomach, the boy knew instinctively now that the bullying would not stop unless he took action . . . immediately.

"After I kick his face in," the boy yelled back, "I'm going to beat the crap out of you!"

The creep, who was bigger than the boy, just smiled and then quickly turned his head the other way without responding. He backed down. This revelation was not missed on the boy, and a plan began to form when he found out that the bully's locker was right outside this classroom.

Finally, the school bell rang, proclaiming the end of the last class of the tortuous day. The boy was determined to at least try to change his misfortune and waited patiently by the bully's locker as the rumor of a new fight spread through the halls like wildfire.

Then the moment of truth came. The boy saw the bully walking toward his locker, but there was something different about him. The thug kept his head down as if to avoid eye contact with the boy.

"Hey, I want a rematch!" shouted the boy.

The bully opened his locker but said nothing, so the boy taunted him some more. Finally, when it was clear that the bully was losing whatever respect he might have from the onlookers, he suddenly threw down his books and charged the boy. A perfect sidekick sent the bully crashing back into the locker, and then something strange happened. The blow did not faze the bully at all. In fact, it just made him madder. He charged again, and this time the fight ended up on the floor, as most fights do.

Unfortunately for the boy, the bully was a former school wrestler, and the boy quickly found himself beneath the bully. He had to improvise quickly or it would be lights out. The words of the boy's hero, Bruce Lee, ran through his mind: *Adapt to the fight.* So he started to pinch the bully, and even though he was pinned on the ground underneath the bully, he quickly gained the leverage he needed and pushed his way to a standing position and broke free.

Punches flew from the left and right. A teacher's voice could be heard shouting from down the hallway, "Stop fighting! Stop fighting!" But those commands weren't even picked up on the radar of the two teen combatants. The boy was getting the worst of the fight, and none of his tae kwon do blocking techniques worked. Suddenly, out of nowhere, the boy shot his fist into the bully's eye. Time froze as the bully flew back several yards in sheer agony. The fight stopped. It was over for the bully. The boy had won.

Although he was pleased to have won, the boy was puzzled. His punch was a completely natural movement, and it was not a movement that he had been taught in his tae kwon do class. In truth, nothing he had been taught in his two years of classes had been effective in a real fight. *Why?* This mystery would plague the boy for several years, and ultimately the answer would change his future.

I know because I *was* that boy.

Violence can strike anywhere. It can strike without warning or provocation in a private religious school, and violence can bring down the Twin Towers on 9/11. This book exposes the many layers of violence in our world so that we can better understand it and hopefully prevent it.

By the way, the school bully tried to intimidate another student who followed my lead and fought back. The school bully was expelled.

URGENT

Chapter
TWO

Keeping Your
Child Safe

It's a Parent's Job to Parent

Chapter **TWO**
Keeping Your Child Safe

*"A child's life is like a piece of paper on which
every person leaves a mark."*
CHINESE PROVERB

Baby boomers can recall a much safer time in the United States when parents and children could almost trust anyone. Still, it was a time where some subjects, such as molestation or incest, were not talked about publicly. *Molestation,* after all, is a nicer word than *child sexual assault,* which is what it really means.

THE BABY-SITTER

Today, we live in a far more open society and a more dangerous one. Most couples do not live close enough to their parents to leave their children in the safe hands of grandma and grandpa. Many couples have to go to external resources to obtain childcare. Unfortunately, the mindset of some parents disregards childcare or baby-sitting as a real job. For them, it's just a matter of finding the right neighbors' teenager, or if they are more affluent, a professional baby-sitter or nanny. In many cases, more thinking and planning goes into the family vacation than into finding a qualified, trustworthy, mature baby-sitter.

As a parent, you need to realize that the baby-sitter is an employee into whose care you will be entrusting your precious children as well as your possessions when you hand over the keys to your house. Therefore, doesn't it make sense that you select the most qualified person for the job? Someone you can trust with absolute confidence?

You should be able to garner this level of trust whether you hire a baby-sitter or use a home or business daycare provider. Parents sometimes assume that since home or business daycare providers are licensed that they provide safe care. This is not always the case. However, home daycare providers survive by word of mouth and quality of service, which is different than an occasional baby-sitter who just needs some pocket money.

Similarly, business daycare providers can be under scrutiny from coworkers and, in some cases, on-site cameras. This is not to say that problems can't occur in these settings. But it is to say that if these services have been around for several years and have not had complaints issued against them, chances are that they will be safe havens for your child.

As a parent, it is prudent to check any daycare provider's service by:

- talking to present clients.
- cross-checking the names of employees against a sexual offender registry list.
- checking for any code or criminal violations with the police department or the Better Business Bureau (although most small businesses may not be able to afford membership in that organization).
- use your intuition and incorporate any of the steps listed below into your examination of home or business day-care providers.

The Three Steps

There are three steps you should use in the selection process of a baby-sitter: the application, the interview, and the use of your intuition.

When you receive an inquiry for your baby-sitting position from an ad or from networking with your coworkers and friends, you can do a brief interview over the phone if it's someone you don't know. Keep the questions simple, such as the person's availability, prior experience, and age. This gives you a chance to use your intuition to see how the applicant feels. If she passes the initial test, then get her address and send out an application. I use the word *she* to describe the baby-sitter because most baby-sitters are female. It is also important to note that, statistically, males are far more likely than females to assault a child.

1. The Application

Once you've conducted a favorable telephone interview, ask for the person's address for where to send the application. Knowing the neighborhood the baby-sitter is from may tell you something about her background. Keep in mind that while professional baby-sitting services do exist, there is no guarantee that their screening service is better than yours. Consequently, the more research you do, the better prepared you will be to start the selection process with the application.

The application form should include writing space for the applicant's name, address, phone numbers, and the names of references as well as their addresses and phone numbers. Other vital information you should require is to include past dates of service, who to contact in case of an emergency, and whether or not the applicant knows child CPR or has had any medical training that deals with saving children's lives.

Once you receive the application, you can judge the seriousness of the applicant by how comprehensively the questions are answered as well as by how the form looks. From there you can select candidates for the next step in the process.

2. The Interview

Once you have selected the candidates you want to interview, call the people who are listed as references on the application and talk to them. Ask open-ended questions such as "What is Linda like?" and "How long has she been baby-sitting, who has she sat for before, and how do you know her?" Also, ask them if they know anyone else whom you can talk to about the applicant. Once you get that name, call the person up and talk to them.

Questions such as "Does Linda hang around any bad people?" may not get you any straight answers as opposed to open-ended questions such as "Tell me about her friends" and "What does she and her friends like to do?" Another good question is, "How old is her boyfriend?" This question assumes she has a boyfriend even if she doesn't. This helps the person who is being used as a reference to feel at ease in case she has a boyfriend, and the reference person is more likely to open up to you. Also, if she doesn't have a boyfriend, you will get a straight answer. If she has a boyfriend, ask for his age. If Linda is 16 and her boyfriend is 30, you might have a problem. Your antenna should go up, depending on the answers you receive.

Using this interview strategy sends a message to the applicant that you are thorough. There may be some applicants who will be discouraged by this, but this is a good thing. You want what is best for your child and yourself, and you shouldn't worry about hurting the applicant's feelings. On the bright side, this painstaking process will help you worry less when you are away.

After calling all the references, you move on to deciding whom the most promising candidates are for interviewing. While this can be mostly a cerebral process, try to keep in touch with your feelings. A bad feeling can mean a bad choice. After evaluating the feedback from the references, ask yourself whether or not you could trust this person with your child. What intuitive feeling do you get when you ask this?

3. The Questions

When asking questions of the applicant, watch for her reactions. How she reacts will give a good or bad feeling. Listen to your intuition. Here are some key questions you should ask:

- "How do you discipline?"
- "What discipline methods did your parents use?"
- "Did your parents ever use physical punishment?"

Baby-sitters who were physically punished as children may have a predilection to physically punish as well. Moreover, she may use the same method that was used on her.

- "In your experience, have you ever come across a child who was physically abused or sexually molested? If yes, what did you do about it? Did you report it to the police?"
- "What do you like about this work?"

- "Have you taken care of younger siblings?"
- "What don't you like about this line of work?"
- "Describe the best baby-sitting experience you have ever had."
- "Describe the worst baby-sitting experience you have ever had."
- "What would you do if the lights in the house go out?"
- "What would you do if the child gets sick?"
- "What would you do if the child stopped breathing?"
- "What would you do if the child began to choke?"
- "Tell me about a problem in your life and how you solved it."
- "Tell me about a problem in your life and how someone helped you with it."
- "What do you think of drugs and alcohol?"
- "Do you have a best friend? Tell me about your relationship with him or her."
- "What would you do if a child played with themselves or did an inappropriate act?"
- "What would you do if a child asked you to keep a secret from the parents?"
- "How do you break up fights between siblings?"
- "Have you been trained in child CPR?"
- "Can we test you for drugs?"
- "Do you personally know people whom you would not allow around our child or children in general? Who is this person?"
- "Do you have a boyfriend? What is your relationship with him? Will he be visiting you when you are baby-sitting?"

These questions probe for maturity and responsibility. If an applicant talks little about her good experiences and a lot about her bad ones, that is a clue. Also, if she uses negative terms such as *brat* to describe her experience with a child, you should dismiss her.

If at anytime you feel you are not getting a complete answer, feel free to use the silent treatment. Don't say anything unless you hear more from the applicant.

Finally, the applicant should ask you a few questions. Specifically, questions that explore what your rules are, if the children have any medical conditions, what activities you recommend for the children to do, and what television programs the children should or should not watch all demonstrate a good deal of responsibility. If the applicant does not ask these types of questions, you need to beware.

The Rules
Once you have settled on a candidate, it's time to tell her the rules, such as:

- Don't steal.
- Don't take the kids out of the house.
- Don't bathe the kids.

Establish your rules, make them crystal clear, and never allow them to be changed.

Then show the baby-sitter the circuit breaker panel and teach her how to fix the breakers if they go off. If your house has a fuse box, show her how to change burned out fuses. Show her the fire extinguisher, and make sure she knows how to operate it. Tell her about the smoke alarm protocols. Show her the child medical release form and give her the relevant contact numbers.

One final piece of advice: if you have the finances available, purchase a camera that can be hidden and set it up. Not only will this give you an added peace of mind, but it can be a valuable source of evidence if your child is somehow hurt or harmed.

One of the best books on the subject of protecting children and teenagers is called *Protecting the Gift* by Gavin de Becker. This book is highly insightful and easy to read, and I highly recommend that you read it.

PUBLIC PLACES

In every parent's life there comes a time when the child must venture into the public. The key is to have the child prepared well enough to deal with whatever negative situations come along. To this extent, here are a number of tips:

- Because anyone can buy a badge and give the appearance of a policeman or a security person, tell your child to seek out a woman if they become lost. Statistically, a woman is less likely to harm them than a man.

- When you tell a child that certain men will harm them, they picture an unshaven bum and not a man in a suit, and that's a problem.

- For every person in public places who might hurt your child, there are thousands who won't.

- A child trained to approach strangers correctly is less likely to become a victim than a child who is taught to never talk to strangers.

- To train your child to talk to strangers, ask your child to pick out a stranger, approach them, and ask them for the time of day or for directions to a particular place. Afterward, ask your child why they chose that particular person, if they felt comfortable with that person, and if they felt that person felt comfortable with them.

- Teach your children that situations can make seemingly safe locations dangerous. If a child is told that the mall is a dangerous place, but the child spends lots of time there without feeling threatened, they will disregard the message. If you describe the situations at the mall that open the door to danger, such as talking with a man who offers them something for free, you help focus their attention on specifics that won't be forgotten.

- Dress your children in highly visible clothing that will allow you to spot them in a crowd.

- Before you go into a public place, agree on a specific place to meet if you get separated.

What Your Child Should Know Before They Go Out

- Tell your child that if a man, any man, starts to talk to them or come close to them, they should run to a safe place and/or yell for help. They should not talk to or respond to men regardless of how harmless they appear or if they claim to need some type of help.

- Tell the child to always stay a good distance from any man, and if for some reason they are grabbed, they should yell "He's not my daddy" and fight back. The best way they can fight back is to do so naturally—bite, scratch, punch, and kick, which they already know how to do without training. Children may not remember choreographed movements or memorized techniques when they are afraid. Children just need a parent's okay to fight back.

- Define a *stranger* to a child as anyone whom the child does not know and/or someone they get a bad feeling from. Sometimes they may get a bad feeling from a relative or a known person in a position of authority. Your child should know that every time they get a bad feeling about someone, regardless of who the person is, they should tell you.

- Some strangers may pretend that they are the father of a child whom your child knows. They say they'll call their child on a cell phone and have them talk to yours, but this is just a trick to get the child into their hands as soon as they come close to the cell phone.

- Their home address and phone numbers.

- To get away from anyone who makes them feel uncomfortable.

- That they can always tell you anything, regardless of how bad it is.

- It's okay to say no to adults.

- It's okay to not do what adults tell them if they're alone and if what's being asked will harm or hurt them.

- Go to a woman to ask for help.

- How to say what's wrong.

- It's okay to scream and yell if they are in trouble.

- It's okay to run from people who want to harm them.

- It's okay to scratch, bite, hit, and kick people who are hurting them and if someone is touching them in places they don't want to be touched.

- It's okay to yell "This is not my father!" when someone tries to grab them or is holding them against their will.

- It's okay to yell even if someone tells them not to yell.

- That when someone tells them to not tell you something, make sure they do tell.

- When someone says that something is a secret, they should always tell you.

- Don't believe someone who says, "Do as you're told, or I'll hurt you."

- Have a safe word that only they and people they know they can trust to pick them up from school can use.

- Never leave an area with someone they don't know even if that someone is ordering them to go.

- Give your child a laminated card that contains all the necessary phone numbers on it and tape fifty cents to the back of it for emergency use at a pay phone.

- If your child is going to walk to school, go with them and study every possible route. If you get a bad feeling from a particular route, tell your child to not follow it. Also, if the child is small for their age, they should go in a group, and you should know the names and contact information for all the group members. And never allow very small children to walk to school alone. The criterion for being too small to go out alone is this: if the father can pick the child up and easily tuck them under their arm without them being able to escape.

- Develop your child's intuition by pointing to strangers and asking them if they would trust that stranger to help them, and if not, why not. You can even turn this into a game for the child.

- If the child is old enough or mature enough for a cell phone, get them one. Program the cell phone so that hitting one number can speed dial to 911, and train the child to use it. Even if a child is kidnapped, they can reach in their pocket and hit that button. This is another game you can play with them as well, so that even without seeing the cell phone they know which number to push.

AT HOME

Many parents are concerned about determining the appropriate age when a child may be left at home. The main concern should not necessarily be their age but rather maturity and necessity. Ideally, a child should never be left home alone, but because of unforeseen circumstances it can happen. Consequently, here are some of the actions a parent can take:

- If a child is left all alone at home, the child should never respond to a knock on the door or answer the door, regardless of who is outside.

- Even if there is an adult in the house, the child should not answer the door. Children may be too small to see through a peephole to verify a person's identity, and criminals are good at giving convincing reasons to enter a home. Some may even dress up as authority figures and carry badges.

- A child left at home should have the ability to contact the parents as quickly as possible as well as know the emergency numbers for the police and fire departments.

- Should a fire or other dangerous situation occur in the home, the child should have a safe house or apartment in the neighborhood to which they can run.

While nothing has a 100 percent guarantee, the more precautions a parent takes the safer the child becomes.

BULLIES

When Sally found out that her son was being bullied at school, she enrolled him in a jujitsu class, so he could defend himself. She felt that if she intervened in some way he would be far worse off. Her son, Brad, learned quickly in his jujitsu class and felt confident that he could fight the bully, if it became necessary.

The chance soon arose. As the bully began to intimidate and push Brad around, Brad did exactly as he'd been taught and executed a perfect takedown, causing the bully to smack the concrete. But no sooner had he dropped the bully than the bully's 10-plus gang members tore into Brad and hospitalized him.

While hoping to instill confidence in her son, Sally made two mistakes. The first was not getting the school authorities involved, and the second was having her son learn from someone who was more oriented in teaching a sport rather than self-defense.

Preventing violence in school requires a multiprong approach. It involves getting the school officials involved. Many schools now have security guards who can keep an eye out for trouble, but they need to know what trouble may occur. Parents should use all the tools at their disposal to keep their child safe, even if it means getting the police, teachers, and other parents involved.

Having a child learn proper self-defense and not sport martial art provides the parent with the peace of mind that the child has a backup plan, whether they are in or out of school. However, parents need to know what works and what doesn't work. For instance, most of today's martial arts come from a culture that teaches a person to only deal with one attacker at a time. This simply doesn't work in the real world where a person may face multiple assailants attacking at the same time. The only self-defense that has a proven track record in dealing with multiple attackers is a Russian martial art called Systema (The System), which is currently being used by the Russian special forces because of its effectiveness.

How can a parent make a distinction between a sport and a self-defense martial art? In today's world it is hard to distinguish one from another as many martial artists advertise that what they teach is self-defense. Some teachers who teach a sport martial art do tell their students what works as a self-defense and what doesn't, while others don't. And others don't know realistic self-defense applications at all.

While I deal with this more extensively in Chapter Eleven, "Martial Myths Exposed," here are a few clues that will allow you to discover the truth. If a martial art is a sport, they generally will:

- Participate in tournaments.
- Teach mostly one-on-one defenses rather than defenses against group attacks.
- Be focused mostly on cardiovascular development, fitness, and discipline rather than self-defense.
- Do a lot of practice on striking pads instead of striking each other.
- Select people of the same height, weight, and skill level to practice with each other.

- Not teach how to avoid physical confrontations without using force.

- Not teach methods that allow a smaller individual to bring down a larger one.

- Not teach defenses against group attacks.

- Not teach defenses against grabs, locks, chokes, and ground attacks both from an individual and a group scenario.

- Not teach defenses against knives and guns.

- Not teach proper use of body mechanics.

- Not teach proper use of breathing.

- Not teach awareness and intuition development.

What makes the parent's job even more difficult is that some of the martial arts stemming from karate were created originally for children to provide discipline, physical fitness, and fairness. While these qualities are admirable, what they don't teach is proper self-defense techniques. There were a number of reasons for this. The original Okinawa karate techniques were potentially deadly, and at that time they didn't want children to know neck snapping techniques. The technology was not developed to have effective protective gear. Consequently, the children were taught the same movements or "kata" as adults, but with different applications so they wouldn't hurt themselves in practice. For example, the movements that are classified as high blocks, middle blocks, or low blocks are really not blocks but a combination of strikes and takedowns. In reality, most of them are offensive moves and not defensive ones.

One of the most prominent forms of this original or traditional karate is found under the Kyusho-Jitsu (Pressure Point Fighting) umbrella and is called Ryukyu kempo. The forms or kata connected with this Jitsu (fighting) are used to map out pressure points on the human body in order to subdue attackers (sometimes by knockout). Two of the most famous teachers of this Okinawa military system are George Dillman and Chris Thomas.

Not all martial arts are based on the karate model, and some focus primarily on ground submissions or joint maneuvers. Still, if the fight goes to the ground, the defender may have only a few seconds to subdue the attacker before the attacker's crew is on top of them, such as in Sally's son's case. Other martial arts may focus on only one aspect of self-defense, such as joint-locking techniques. This may be fine against one individual, but it won't work against a group that is striking, punching, and kicking the victim all at the same time.

This is important for parents to know, because if they are told by a martial arts instructor that classes against group attacks are taught, they need to find out if the instructor means that the person being attacked is defending against one person at a time or a group at a time. Bullies and their crews aren't going to be polite and follow rules. They will attack at the same time, and there are no rules.

And bullying can happen to girls, too. Jennifer was twelve when another girl in her art class threatened to beat her up. Frightened and not knowing what to do, she asked her father for help that evening. Fortunately, her father had a background in dealing with issues such as this. He told her to challenge the girl to a one-on-one match after school, and to challenge her in front of her gang. The wording she was supposed to use was very specific. She was to tell the girl: "Just me and you out back after school."

Needless to say, Jennifer was very frightened. She tried to believe her father was right, but that didn't stop the upset feeling she had. When the next art class began, the bully and her gang started in on Jennifer, who reached down deep inside herself and made the challenge. The bully quickly agreed. As the school bell rang, Jennifer started to become more frightened. She made her way down the long corridor, out the door, and into the schoolyard where she was supposed to fight. No one was there yet, so she waited. Ten minutes passed and still no bully. She began to become more confident. Another 10 minutes passed and still no bully. Finally, after waiting for 30 minutes, she started to walk home. At the next art class, the bully and her crew showed up, but this time they didn't pick on Jennifer or anyone else in the class.

In this case, as opposed to Sally's story, Jennifer's father was qualified to come up with the appropriate response, which had nothing to do with learning a physical defense tactic.

Rather, it involved the use of psychology. Effective self-defense involves not only the physical movements but also awareness, intuition, correct breathing, proper body mechanics, relaxation, as well as psychology. It is always best to prevent a fight rather than have to take part in one, regardless of how much self-defense training you have had.

Still, there are a number of concerns any parent would have about Jennifer's situation, despite this happy ending. Weapons are finding there way more easily into the classroom. Here the bully didn't have a record of using knives or guns. In fact, her ability to manipulate people just came from the fear of an attack rather than actual violence, and Jennifer's father knew that.

But what if the other girl had a knife and was willing to use it? Would the story be different if the bully lives in the neighborhood? What would have happened if the school authorities were involved? While this instance ended peacefully, each incident is different, and there is no formula for guaranteed solutions.

As schoolchildren mature, for the most part they want to take things on by themselves, therefore having good communication between parent and child is essential. It is also important for the parents to be involved with the school. While this scenario did not involve school authorities, it is always advisable that the school counselor or other proper authorities know that a child is a bully. Unfortunately, the bottom line sometimes is that the children will take matters into their own hands, whether in school or out.

Bullies, however, act in a specific way. They usually target students who are loners or don't seem to fit in, because one of the last things a bully wants to deal with is someone who has a crew of friends. Therefore, if a student joins a club or clubs, they increase their chances of not being picked on, especially if they are always walking around with a group of friends. If the student becomes a target of a bully, all the friends have to do is put their hand on the victim's shoulders and just walk him away from the bully without saying a word. This will leave the bully target-less.

If a bully lives in the neighborhood, the child should feel open about discussing any bullying incident with their parents. Then the parents can contact the parents of the bully to resolve the issue. If this doesn't work, the police should be called. While some police might not wish to get involved in a bullying scenario, when the terminology used to explain the incident to the police contains such catch phrases as "attempted assault," "assault," or "attempted murder," their resolve to assist increases.

URGENT

Chapter
THREE

Keeping Teenagers Safe

Communication Is Key

Chapter **THREE**
Keeping Teenagers Safe

"We real cool.
We Left school.
We Lurk late.
We Strike straight.
We Sing sin.
We Thin gin.
We Jazz June.
We Die soon."
GWENDOLYN BROOKS

There are many dangers that face teenagers these days. In his book *Protecting the Gift,* Gavin de Becker states that "gunshot wounds are now the leading cause of death for boys in America." This statement, while horrific, illustrates the change in times, attitudes, and easy access to guns from the 1950s to the present.

For parents, the concept of bullying they most likely relate to is one that dates back to the time when they were in school.

This may mean that they see bullying as a one-on-one issue with participants being of close to equal weight and without any other considerations. For the most part, this notion is pretty close to fiction. Teenagers can be bullied by people twice their size, and some have guns and are in gangs.

The best weapon a parent has in these circumstances is an open line of communication with their child. If your child wants to talk to you, put everything else on the sidelines, including work. Opt for adopting a life ethic rather than a work ethic. Transferring work to the back burner is very hard to do in American society, especially when both parents work and that work often involves extremely long hours. This can lead to miscommunications and feelings by children that their own parents don't care about them. Teenagers often won't demand your time, and they may be reluctant to talk with you about a bully because they are trying to prove to themselves that they can handle situations. But this very reluctance and taking matters into their own hands, if taken to the extreme, can lead tragically to Columbine-like school massacres.

THE BULLY KILLERS

Victims of bullies are fighting back, but they are using guns, pipe bombs, and other devices instead of their fists to do so. Both instigators of the Columbine massacre were bullied, as has been true of the instigators in many other school-related shootings by students. But instead of talking to their parents about it, the two boys in Columbine formed a bond with each other. They apparently endured bullying for years before crafting their final horrific solution.

So how can you tell if your teenager is prone to commit these types of acts? In *Protecting the Gift,* author Gavin de Becker notes predictive signals that occur prior to major acts of violence. They are:

- alcohol and drug abuse
- addiction to media products
- a sense of aimlessness
- a fascination with weapons and violence
- experience with guns
- access to guns
- sullen, angry, depressed (SAD)
- seeking status and worth through violence
- threats of violence or suicide
- rejection and humiliation
- media provocation

HELPING HAMLET

Bullies and bully killers both act out learned aggression, which usually stems from their life experiences. This could mean being exposed to domestic violence and believing that such behavior is normal. The old adage that the apple doesn't fall far from the tree surely applies here.

So if we know what can cause this violence, how do we prevent it? How do we help Hamlet? More specifically, if your family doesn't have these problems, what can you do to see that the product of these problems doesn't impact your teenager at school?

- Besides having open lines of communication between parent and child, the student must be able to identify the signals of potential danger and tell parents and school authorities as well.

- Every school should have psychologists or counselors on hand to deal with this danger.

- Many students internalize stress from home as well as from school and need a healthy outlet where they can bond beyond their cliques. Parents should encourage and support their teen in accessing these outlets.

- Overworked parents and overstressed kids are a recipe for disaster. Ideally, corporations should follow the European model and give employees at least four weeks of vacation each year. But the key for parents is that they find time for their children, and to stop what they're doing and really be there. No matter how busy a day is, parents should find time to spend with their children over the dinner table, even if it's just for dessert. Focus on their needs, and you'll get a clear picture of what's on their heart.

- The biggest villain in the world today is stress. The more ways you and your family can get rid of it the better. This may mean cutting down on some sport activity or a work project just to spend a weekend together as a family. Slowing down can help people live better.

TEEN SUICIDE

Teenagers often turn inward when feeling rejected or unwanted. Consequently, they may end up believing that their only form of release is suicide. The American Academy of Child and Adolescent Psychiatry provides this list of symptoms that may occur before a deadly suicide attempt:

- Change in eating and sleeping habits.
- Saying things such as "I won't be a problem much longer," "It's no use," or "Nothing matters."
- A marked personality change.
- Drug and alcohol use.
- Rebellious behavior, running away, or violent actions.
- Ongoing boredom, difficulty in concentrating, or a decline in the quality of work.
- Loss of interest in pleasurable activities.
- Frequent complaints about physical symptoms related to emotions, such as headaches and fatigue.
- Putting their affairs in order, such as giving away their favorite possessions, cleaning their room, and throwing away important belongings.

When you see these symptoms occur in your child or even someone else's child, seek professional help as soon as you can. Alert your child that it's important for them to tell you if they see these symptoms in one of their schoolmates—it could mean the difference between life and death. This allows you to talk to other parents about this as well as the school or police authorities.

URGENT

Chapter
FOUR

What to Teach
Your Daughter
About Dating

Being Safe Means Being Prepared

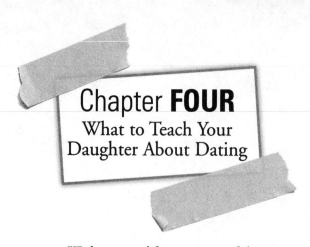

Chapter **FOUR**
What to Teach Your Daughter About Dating

> *"To be prepared for war is one of the most*
> *effectual means of preserving peace."*
> GENERAL GEORGE WASHINGTON

My first inclination in titling this chapter was to call it "What to Teach Your Daughter About Fighting." Having taught self-defense techniques to hundreds of females, the toughest roadblock to personal safety often is gender conditioning. Girls are taught, more precisely conditioned, not to fight. They don't want to hurt anyone, even when their own safety may depend on it. This changes radically when they become mothers. They then become the fiercest warriors on earth to protect their child. The key is to instill that same sense of value and self-worth in your daughter.

In many of my seminars, I ask women to raise their hand if they would use a particularly horrific physical technique to defend themselves—one that would truly hurt an assailant.

About 98 percent of the respondents reply that they would not, even if it meant losing their own life. Then I ask them if they would use that same technique if they were forced to protect their child. One hundred percent of the respondents signify that they would.

One of the best ways to instill this self-worth is through realistic self-defense training. Stay away from those martial arts that look as though they are more closely related to sport rather than to self-defense that works on the street. You're not looking for training that teaches physical fitness and discipline. You want training that teaches real self-defense. It could be a lifesaver.

Keep in mind that when you are looking at self-defense training options for a child who is seven years old, for instance, you want a program that has physical contact without the use of padding and that teaches how to deal specifically with dangerous situations, but not by punching in the air or by having contests with lots of rules. You're not looking for a program that focuses on discipline or cardiovascular fitness. You're looking for a program that will make your child comfortable with physical struggle and physical contact against one or more individuals. Oftentimes the best defense is just letting your child know that it is okay to scratch, punch, kick, bite, and scream at anyone who intends to harm them, touch them in a private place, or move them to another location.

Once she has absorbed this new defensive conditioning, it's likely that it won't be her favorite hobby once she starts to date. Still, having practiced self-defense and not sport martial art, she will have a sense of how much damage she can do. And she'll have a higher developed self-worth. In other words, she's more likely to fight back when it is necessary.

Prior to actually dating, boys and girls may tend to experiment with each other. Older parents can recall the term "playing house." If this concerns you as a parent, and it should, two things can help—open and honest communication and constant vigilance. Again, nothing is a 100 percent solution, but if you tell your daughter that it's healthy to be curious but she should come to you if she has any questions, that may help alleviate some of the concern. Don't just hold your breath and hope that nothing bad happens. Take an active role, talk to your kids, and give them the information and understanding they need. If you give them a healthy, age-appropriate perspective on sex, you eliminate much of the mystery about sex as well as the reasons why so many kids get into trouble.

SOME MEN ARE DOGS

While preparing your daughter for the dating scene should be more than a laundry list chat, it often isn't. It is your responsibility to instruct your daughter on the seriousness of dating and of the qualities she should be looking for in a young man. There's no one who can influence her more than you can as a parent, and hopefully the wisdom you impart to her will keep her from situations with men that require her to act in self-defense. But it is irresponsible to not prepare her for the possibility.

So here are some key concepts that she needs to know in regards to self-defense:

- No one has the right to force you to do something you don't want to do or don't want them to do to you.
- Some men are dogs, and some are good at disguising it. If you discover the man you are with is a dog, you must realize there is only one way they understand what you say: to get a man to do something or stop doing something you have to use short commands as you would when training a dog. These men see long sentences as a way to wear down your objections.
- Using commands, such as "Stop!" or "No!" or "Get out!" gets better results than being polite, if being polite didn't work.
- It's okay to raise your voice when using commands.
- Don't smile when you say no, because some of these men won't take you seriously.
- Swearing is okay, too! Some men won't think you're serious unless you swear.
- Always have a cell phone with you and set the speed dial to 911 or the equivalent emergency police number.

- Tell your parents if something bad happened on the date.
- Always tell the truth.
- Know it's okay to hit, bite, scratch, kick, punch, and gouge your date if he is not listening to you, not respecting you, and is doing what you don't want him to do.
- Know that some men will try to slip date rape drugs into your drink to render you defenseless. These drugs may also be added into ice cubes, so be wary of whom you trust at a party. Keep your drink with you at all times, even if you have to use the bathroom. It's always good to go to a party with female friends who won't desert you. Agree together that even if one of you meet a cute boy, you won't go out with him alone that night.
- When you go on vacation, whether in a place you're familiar with or in a foreign place such as Aruba, make sure that in the evening you never get separated from your female friends or family members, and that all of you return to your hotel together.
- Give your daughter emergency money to use if she gets into trouble, and tell her that you love her very much. There is nothing more powerful than giving your daughter the sense that you love her unconditionally.

URGENT

How to Keep Your Family Safe at Home

Plan, Practice, and Prepare

Chapter **FIVE**
How to Keep Your Family Safe at Home

"To have the arts of peace, but not the arts of war, is to lack courage. To have the arts of war, but not the arts of peace, is to lack wisdom."
HAYASHI RAZAN, 1583–1657

What if I told you that a secret weapon exists that can sense a crime before it starts? What if I told you that this weapon could even add up to two years to your lifespan as well as help keep your family safe? Interested? Well, the secret weapon I'm talking about isn't actually a secret. It's a guard dog. Actually, it's two guard dogs.

Professional guard dogs can be expensive, sometimes ranging from $2,500 to $45,000, so for the average family, getting a good pedigreed dog that has a well developed protective instinct, such as a German shepherd, Doberman pinscher, rottweiler, Dutch shepherd, or a Belgian Malinois, may be just the ticket. Actually, in some cases, it's even possible to get by with just an ordinary mutt for protection purposes. When looking for a dog that will be protective of you and your family, it is good to interact with it first and get a sense of its intelligence and instincts.

Jane was a single mom living in a second-story apartment with her son. It was after midnight when she suddenly awoke to the sounds of barking and snarling. By the time she found the reason for the disturbance, her son's American terrier was voraciously gnawing on the ankle of an intruder, who was doing all he could to get away. The dog definitely made a lasting impression on the criminal.

When considering their home's defense, most people's first thought is that of installing a security alarm or buying a gun. Either of these methods, however, brings several potential problems with them. While an alarm system can work effectively in protecting against an ordinary thief, it can be breached by an experienced criminal. Sometimes, even the threat of an alarm, such as an alarm system sticker on a window, may deter entry by an inexperienced thief. However, an experienced or desperate crook knows that the police or security forces need time to get to your house. In some communities, such as where I live in Milwaukee, Wisconsin, it has been debated that the police would not respond to burglar alarms due to an overwhelming number of false alarms. Plus, in some cases the neighbors may either be too far away, asleep, or not care if your alarm goes off.

According to Sanford Strong, the author of *Strong on Defense,* "Eighty percent of all crime occurs in the three places where you spend most of your time—your home or adjacent to it, your place of work and its parking lot, and the public routes that you travel regularly, including where you jog, walk, or rollerblade." Armed with this knowledge, it only makes sense to develop a plan of action to accommodate these circumstances.

There are two types of home intruders—burglars and armed intruders. Burglars wait until you are gone to enter your home, which is why some people like to leave the lights on and music blaring so as to keep burglars out. Home intruders don't care about any of these deterrents. They'll either burst in or use some type of ruse to get you to open the door.

Consequently, when you and your family find an armed intruder with a gun in your house:

- React immediately.
- Have a plan that includes a safety code word that directs family members to take appropriate action, which usually means that the spouse and/or the children flee to a specified neighbor's house while the other spouse physically attacks the intruder. It also means that one spouse may end up hurt or even dead. Still, it's better than the other option, in which the criminal uses the threat of violence and locks up the most physically able spouse in the closet while he goes on to rape, torture, and/or kill

the rest of the family. There are no perfect solutions in this scenario, and everything is situational. This is the last resort, if the robber has taken your goods but wants to hurt your family, too.

- Since home intruders first seek to control the adults, they often do this by pointing a gun at the wife or child and making threats. If this happens, say these words with forceful intent to the intruder: "You can have anything you want in the house. But if you hurt my child or my wife, I will have nothing left to lose, and I will kill you. I've killed before, and I will do it again." It doesn't matter if you've killed or not. What matters is that the intruder doesn't know that.

- Try to get close to the intruder so you can jump him. To get close to an armed intruder, ask questions that appeal to their greed and demand a response. For example, say to him, "I have a bank card. Would you like to go with me now to pull out some money?" The intruder's response will be either no, yes, or he'll ask you how much you have in the account. Either way, as you inch closer, your family can prepare to bolt when you give them an agreed upon signal. While you approach, you can keep your hands up, but try to keep them under the position of the intruder's gun. When an intruder answers a question, about half his focus is on pulling the trigger while the other half is on providing you with an answer.

This gives you an opportunity to move close enough to say the family code word, so that the rest of your family can bolt to safety as you jump the intruder. As to the manner of disarming the intruder, that is best studied personally under a certified instructor. If this is not possible, one of the best DVDs I've seen is *Gun Disarming* by Vladimir Vasiliev, which can be ordered from www.russianmartialart.com.

- Do not do what the intruder tells you to do. The intruder's most common method of operation is to separate the husband by threatening the wife and kids, so that the intruder can tie the husband down or lock him in a closet. Do not let this happen.

- A good escape plan will include multiple routes to leave the house in the event the intruder has one route blocked, such as a hallway. Although not a popular choice, the spouse must decide if this is the opportunity to fight back.

- Make all your survival decisions ahead of time and practice your escape drills often with your children and spouse, and make sure everyone participates. Practice should include yelling and screaming when escaping to attract attention and discourage the intruder. When you get one person out of the house, the intruder's will power may begin to break. In most cases, it will be the child who flees first.

- At the sound of the code word, all family members should scream and shout. Depending on the circumstances, the family member designated as the one to attack the intruder should make a decision as to whether to attack while the rest of the family escapes or escape with the family.

- Having good house lights, locks, alarms, and dogs make a huge difference.

- For second-story homes use a knotted rope to escape through the window if necessary.

- Always have a mindset of *I will survive.* You can even say this over and over to yourself when placed in dangerous circumstances.

- Breathing and relaxation are two key elements in dealing with fear, anxiety, and adrenaline. Taking breaths through the nose and exhaling through the mouth can foster the necessary relaxation.

WEAPONS IN THE HOME

According to Sanford Strong, guns are by far the most ineffective weapon to have in the home as a means of defense. He points out that in America:

- Eighty-three percent of suicides by gun are committed with a firearm kept primarily for home protection.

- Ten percent of all loaded guns kept in American homes for protection end up being used to kill a family member during the heat of an argument.

- On average, one child per day is killed while playing with a loaded gun.

Reverend Mike got transferred to a new parish and found his home right next to a notorious drug house. Although the reverend had actually practiced martial arts for many years, he felt he needed to buy a gun, so he did.

For five weeks he regularly left the house to practice target shooting. One day as he was going to his bedroom to pick up his gun and head for the shooting range, he heard his eight-year-old daughter ask, "Daddy, where are you going?" Before he could respond, his six-year-old son said, "Shooting." Then Reverend Mike froze midway in the bedroom as he heard his son say, "The gun's in the closet." The next day Reverend Mike got rid of the gun.

Eventually, the drug house was busted up, and nobody was hurt. To this day, Reverend Mike knows that he made the right choice.

Why didn't the reverend keep the gun in a safe? Who knows? Perhaps with a criminal element nearby, he wanted quick access to it. Still, nobody can ignore the fact that far too many children find access to guns in their homes with devastating results.

What is it like to be woken in the middle of the night by an intruder? Picture yourself suddenly awakening and trying to drive someone else's car in the pitch black on a road while speeding at 75 miles an hour. You first have to find the controls and figure out how they work before you can get things under control. Now, picture yourself being awakened by an intruder in the middle of the night. You have to find your gun, unlock it, load it, and be calm enough to fire it at someone who might also be armed and fire back. Now, add a spouse and children into this deadly mix.

Despite all these factors, many people still feel it is better to have a gun or shotgun than to face a criminal with just your bare hands?

I maintain that the best solution is to make sure that you are not faced with this reality in the first place. This also means:

- Being part of or starting a neighborhood watch.
- Getting guard dogs.
- Going through a civilian police academy.
- Having well-lit corridors and parking lots if you live in an apartment, or having motion-sensitive or light-sensitive lighting if you live in a house.
- Making sure that the police know when you are going on vacation and leaving lights on a timer so as to give everyone else the illusion that you are still at home.
- If you go on a vacation, consider getting a reliable house sitter as well as informing your local police department.

Even if your weapon is pepper spray, you still have to function under these extreme circumstances. Therefore, the best home defense weapon is a pair of protective dogs. While an intruder might feel brazen enough to take on one dog, two well trained dogs will make any intruder think twice. Again, if you can prevent a crime from occurring, it is *far better* than engaging in a gun battle with loved ones in the house.

Deception has always been important in military strategy, and it is no different when fighting a war on crime at home. If you, for some reason, can't have a dog, you can still create the illusion of having one by:

- Making sure there is a huge dog bowl outside your house with dog food strewn about it and with a name such as "Monster," "Jaws," or "Killer" written on it.
- Having *Beware of Vicious Dogs* signs posted.
- Adding a few very large deer bones next to the dog dish that's outside your house is an especially good idea if you live in the country.
- Having an alarm that sounds like a dog barking when someone attempts to break in.

Deception techniques work best on criminals who are not from your surrounding area. Those who are from your area or stake out your home for a number of weeks will see through these methods. Consequently, this brings us back to the original strategy of owning a good dog or dogs that have inherent protective instincts.

DOMESTIC VIOLENCE

Upon reporting to 911 that her estranged husband had threatened her and was on the way to her house, Mia was informed that the police could not be sent because the restraining order she had against him had expired. Within minutes, Mia, her three children, and her estranged husband were all dead.

Mia is actually a composite of several women whose lives were destroyed by domestic violence. It is no surprise that 75 percent of spousal murders occur after the woman leaves. This makes it imperative to get out of an abusive relationship as soon as possible and to avoid getting into one in the first place all the more important.

So how do you know if you're dating a potential abuser? Here are a few possible indicators:

- He grew up in an abusive and/or violent household.
- He can be controlling.
- He wants to accelerate the relationship into a marriage or living together commitment.
- He has a history of violent behavior.
- He uses his abuse of drugs or alcohol as an excuse for his behavior.
- He can become easily jealous of you.
- Your intuition is telling you so.

While the use of intuition can be effective, those involved in abusive relationships tend to have an intuition blackout. They tend to adopt a set of false beliefs that become their guiding light, such as believing that:

- The abuser will change.
- The abuser is not at fault for his actions.
- They actually deserved the abuse.
- They can actually change the abuser.

Sometimes a victim's ego gets involved when she or he just doesn't want to admit that she or he made a wrong decision in committing to an abusive relationship. So if intuition doesn't work, is there a way to tell if you or someone you love is in an abusive relationship? The answer is yes and can be found in the following quiz.

Does your partner:

- Want to make all your decisions for you?
- Want to control your actions, such as who you see, where you go, and to whom you talk?
- Want to keep you on a tight leash?
- Limit your contact with your friends and family?
- Take your money, make you ask for money, or refuse to give you money?
- Make you scared?

- Verbally abuse you?
- Threaten to take away or hurt your children?
- Blame you for causing him to abuse you?
- Act as though abusing you is no big deal?
- Deny abusing you even after abusing you?
- Embarrass you privately or in the company of others with putdowns or derogatory names?
- Threaten to commit suicide?
- Threaten to destroy your property or pets?
- Intimidate you with guns, knives, or other weapons?
- Shove, slap, hit, or sexually attack you?
- Threaten to kill you?
- Force you to drop charges against him?

If you answered yes to any one of these questions, you may be in an abusive relationship and require professional assistance. You can call a law enforcement agency, domestic abuse hotline, or domestic abuse shelter for help. There is also the National Domestic Violence Hotline at 1-800-799-SAFE, and if you have Internet capability you can obtain more information from the Rape Abuse and Incest National Network (www.rainn.org) as well.

"In the United States, women are killed by intimate partners more often than by any other type of perpetrator, with the majority of these murders involving prior physical abuse," says

Jacquelyn Campbell, Ph.D., R.N., author of *Risk Factors for Femicide*. In fact, a batterer's unemployment, access to guns, and threats of deadly violence are the strongest predictors of female homicide in abusive relationships, according to a study published in the July 2003 issue of *The American Journal of Public Health*.

While there can be a long list of pre-incident indicators associated with spousal violence and homicide, the bottom line is this: if you don't like the relationship you are in, get help. While you may not feel that you are in danger or that being without your partner is worse than being with them, an objective and professional opinion has no downside. Get help, and get it now!

URGENT

How to Be
Safe at Work

Vanquish Violence Through Vision

Chapter **SIX**
How to Be Safe
at Work

"Failing to plan is planning to fail."
BENJAMIN FRANKLIN

I s there someone at work of whom you are frightened?
Well, you might have good reason to be.

A fired letter carrier from the post office in Dana Point, California,
who had been terminated for stalking a female coworker, returned
one day in December 1992, opened fire, and killed a coworker.
Police later learned that the man had killed his mother prior to the
shooting, shot and wounded a woman motorist shortly after it,
and then shot and wounded two customers at an automated teller
machine in an apparent robbery attempt.

Nearly four out of 10 women killed at work are murdered.
According to a report from the U.S. Department of Labor, this
makes murder the leading cause of death for women in the
workplace. Additionally, the National Institute for

Occupational Safety and Health (NIOSH) states that since 1980 at least 750 people per year have been murdered at work. This makes murder the third-leading cause of occupational death overall. Furthermore, in the August 1994 issue of Bureau of Labor Statistics, the U.S. Department of Justice proclaimed the workplace to be the most dangerous place in America.

Although some occupations may be more inherently dangerous, one thing for certain is that workplace violence is making its presence known everywhere. Almost everyone has heard of an incident, whether at their place of work or from the news media. It appears that there are no safe havens.

Violence has even found its way into the healthcare industry. The December 7, 1994 issue of the *Journal of the American Medical Association* reported that there were 106 homicides of healthcare workers between 1980 and 1990, including 27 pharmacists, 26 physicians, 18 nurses, and 17 nurse's aides. In 1992, homicide accounted for 42 percent of work-related deaths among women. Information from the National Victim Center cites recent studies by Northwestern National Life Insurance and NIOSH have identified that the chances are one in four that a worker may be attacked, threatened, or harassed on the job next year.

The impact of workplace violence on employers can be staggering. Six out of 10 incidents of workplace violence occur in private companies. These incidents cost companies $4.2 billion dollars in lost work and legal expenses in 1992, according to the National Safe Workplace Institute. The institute further calculates that the average cost to employers of a single episode of workplace violence can amount to $250,000 in lost work time and legal expenses.

Another survey conducted by the National Safe Workplace Institute also paints a gloomy picture. This survey revealed that out of the 248 security and safety directors surveyed in 27 states, nine out of 10 security directors had knowledge of more than three incidents of men stalking women employees. The survey also stated that of those surveyed, 94 percent acknowledged that domestic violence is a "high" security problem at their companies.

Information from the National Victim Center shows that for every murder there are numerous rapes and assaults that often leave victims battered and disabled. According to the U.S. Department of Justice, husbands and boyfriends, current and former, commit more than 13,000 acts of violence against women in the workplace every year. Additionally, statistics illustrate that 20 percent of all workplace incidents against women involving physical injury were traced to a romantic entanglement that involved either a coworker or outside spouse or boyfriend.

In cases where there are legal injunctions or restraining orders barring perpetrators from going to the victim's home, they enter the workplace in their search for the intended victims.

"Victims' addresses and telephone numbers can be changed but not necessarily their places of employment" reports the National Victim Center.

In their 1993 book, *Violence in Our Schools, Hospitals, and Public Places,* Eugene D. Wheeler and Anthony S. Baron reveal a 1989 study of violence in 300 hospitals surveyed across the nation. It was found that there had been a sharp upswing in assaults, and that half of the assaults took place in the emergency room. Furthermore, a 1991 study of 1,200 emergency room nurses showed that two out of three reported they had been assaulted during their careers.

WHAT EMPLOYERS CAN DO

Employers are becoming more aware of the high costs that violence can cause their companies to suffer in:

- security.
- building repair and clean up.
- business interruptions with customers.
- lost productivity and work time.
- employee turnover.
- salary continuation for those who are injured or traumatized.
- valued employees quitting or retiring early.
- increases in workers' compensation claims, insurance premiums, and medical claims.

- attorney fees, medical care, and psychological care for current employees. It has been estimated that these costs could be as high as 36 billion dollars per year in the United States.

A company has several ways to help prevent violence. The first is through implementing a thorough pre-employment checking mechanism. The second is by having a well-educated security force. The third is by maintaining a well-informed personnel department that encourages employee communication on these issues and sponsors programs to deal with these issues, including self-protection and awareness programs for its employees.

Often, too much emphasis is placed on the interview in making a hiring decision. This is because the interview is a method of determining suitability for a position and acceptability into a specific corporate culture. The potential problem with a standard job interview is that the candidate can lie, and it is very hard to determine the truth unless he or she is hooked up to a lie detector. That's why other independent means, such as calling previous employers to verify information as well as to check on the quality of the person's character, is essential. A good pre-employment check can uncover a potential problem.

Depending on the right-to-privacy laws in your state, employers can search public records for incidents of criminal or civil misconduct. They can also access the Department of Motor Vehicles to see if the candidate's license is current and the driver is in good standing. Most records are now on computer, so checking them has become a lot easier. In fact, failure to do so may lead to accusations of negligent hiring, if something happens later. Employers can also verify an applicant's social security number with the Social Security Administration to make sure he is who he says he is. Most importantly, records that list criminal convictions, judgments, liens, and civil suits are available through a number of online computer services.

Unfortunately, not every potential criminal can be screened. Many people at work can develop mental illness or suffer from depression or other stressors that can put them over the edge well after they have been hired.

While there are those who believe that it is possible to compile data that identifies violence prone behavior, the best test of violent behavior is violent behavior. If there is an employee who stalks or threatens others in the workplace, causing them to fear him, or if there is an employee whose been written up or warned about such behavior, the employer must take immediate and appropriate steps. Some of the best protection for an employer is to take each complaint or employee warning as seriously as possible. Intervention is the best prevention.

Employers can take a number of steps to safeguard employees as well as themselves:

- Provide on-site stress relieving services, such as offering a pilates exercise program, massage, physical training, acupuncture, and/or counseling.

- Provide safety services, such as seminars on violence prevention or self-defense instruction.

- Provide coupons or reimbursement to employees who engage in these or other stress-relieving activities.

- Have a toll-free anonymous service that employees can call if they are aware that someone is becoming dangerous.

- Make an effort to follow up on reports of employees who appear depressed, sullen, and/or angry, commit inappropriate acts, obsessively, romantically pursue other coworkers, exhibit a fascination with violence, guns, and/or a survivalist attitude, and make threats or behave in a threatening manner.

- Recognize and don't tolerate patterns of insubordination, intimidation, sabotage, threats, bullying, manipulations, and actions that cause fear and anxiety.

WHAT EMPLOYEES CAN DO

While the employer has the responsibility to keep the workplace safe, the employer cannot do it without the help of the employee. Preventing violence in the workplace is a two-way street. Employers can only act on information they receive. If an employee feels threatened by another employee, the threatened employee must report it to the appropriate personnel. This includes incidences of domestic violence or stalking as well, because when the perpetrator has threatened to follow the victim or is stalking the victim, the workplace is in danger.

If an employee remains silent about their suspicions about another employee, they must accept the burden for whatever tragedy unfolds.

Employees can help prevent workplace violence when they:

- Report inappropriate behavior.
- Seek help for domestic abuse situations that they may be experiencing either on their own or through employer assistance.
- Make employers aware of potential stalking situations.
- Report incidents of suspicious employee behavior, even if it is just a "gut" feeling.
- Use an anonymous employee tip line or notify Employee Assistance or HR if they suspect or overhear that a violent act may occur or that an employee has stated a desire to commit acts of violence, has obtained a weapon within the last 90 days, talks a lot about weapons, is paranoid, spies on other employees, seems as though he has a huge chip on his shoulder, believes he is unfairly picked on, or is continually depressed.
- Are persistent when an employer doesn't take the necessary precautions, even if it means moving higher up the chain of command, writing and sending a certified letter so as to establish documentation, and, if necessary, contacting the police, media, or an attorney.
- Take measures to reduce their own stress levels, even by

steps as simple as cutting down their caffeine intake by substituting green tea for coffee.

- Take care of themselves emotionally, physically, and spiritually.

- Recognize that they must get professional help and get out of an abusive relationship immediately.

TERMINATION

When an employer makes a determination to terminate the employment of a potentially violent individual, they should:

- Not let it leak out that the employee is going to be fired. Treat them respectfully as a normal employee and not be afraid of them.

- Make the termination immediate so the terminated employee doesn't have to come back the next day. If they have personal items, tell them to go ahead and remove them immediately. Be direct and don't lecture.

- Have security on standby but not in the room where the termination is to take place.

- Give them some input by asking how to deal with their phone calls and mail.

- Make the employee feel better by saying that the job they have is really not helping them to excel. Let them think they are capable person.

- Fire the employee at the end of the day when most workers on that shift have already left the place of work.

- Not fire the employee in your normal office but rather an out of the way place that will give you the opportunity to leave when you must.

- Whenever possible, have a higher level manager with whom the employee has not worked do the firing. A second person, preferably one admired by the employee, should be there as well to help insure that the employee is on good behavior.

- Prior to the firing, and depending on if your state has made carrying a concealed weapon legal, the employer should have signs posted that state weapons are not allowed in the workplace or in the parking lot and enforce this regulation with electronic weapons screeners.

URGENT

How to Be Safe on the Street

The Power Is Within You

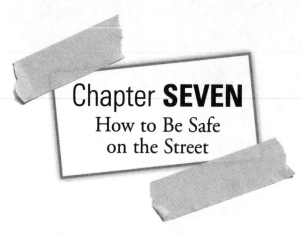

Chapter **SEVEN**
How to Be Safe on the Street

*"Fighting skill should evolve into an unconquerable weapon
that can't be seen until used nor taken away
while its practitioner is alive."*
VLADIMIR VASILIEV

I t has been said that criminals are animals. Indeed, when it comes to attacking people, they certainly can behave as animals. If you have ever seen a nature program where a pack of wolves is searching for a prey, what do the wolves typically seek? They look for the weakest, most defenseless animal they can find. Usually, the animal is very young or old or sick, which means it cannot defend itself. This is the same behavior that most criminals look for in their victims.

Criminals are lazy. They want to choose someone they feel will be an easy victim—someone who won't fight back. Consequently, they look for someone who gives the appearance of a victim.

So what do victims look like? There are at least four qualities of victimhood:

- Victims project low self-esteem.
- Victims usually walk with their head down.
- Victims look unaware of their surroundings.
- Victims communicate an attitude of surrender through their posture and body language.

This falls perfectly within one part of the criminal's formula. Crimes happen when criminal intent meets opportunity. So we can say that criminal intent + opportunity = crime.

Recently in the Wisconsin county where I live, a woman was assaulted by five attackers. This incident happened in the early hours of the morning outside a convenience store in a bad neighborhood, which is a setting that provides criminals with the perfect opportunity to exploit the weak. As the woman left the store, they surrounded her, and one of the assailants pulled out a weapon and told her to come with them.

Unfortunately, the woman went with the assailants and was assaulted. While I cannot say whether or not she demonstrated the four qualities of victimhood, I can surmise that she was at least unaware of her surroundings, or she wouldn't have been there at such a dangerous time.

This brings me to a very important point. If anyone ever pulls out a weapon and tells you to come with them, especially after they've robbed you, don't go. After they've taken your money, the only reason they want you to move is so that they can hurt or kill you. Even before they rob you, breathe, relax, and try to get a sense of whether you can run away safely. I recommend that you always carry a "drop wallet" that has a lot of one dollar bills in it. If your assailant pulls a weapon, throw down the "drop wallet" and try to escape.

Every criminal situation is unique. Robbers may want to move you to obtain money from another place. However, remember that if they just took your money, or if you're out on the street, they may want more from you than your money.

REFUSE TO LOOK LIKE A VICTIM

There are at least seven ways to project an "I'm not a victim" look:

1. *Walk engaged.* This means to walk with your head held up, shoulders squared, and with purpose.

2. *Return eye contact normally.* Let your eyes briefly meet to acknowledge the person coming toward you. Don't stare at the people looking at you, and don't walk looking down at the sidewalk. This may vary in large cities such as New York, where the norm is to look away.

3. *Walk as though you belong.* Even if you are uncertain of where you are, don't look rushed but walk at a confident and comfortable pace. Oftentimes criminals will attack you if you look lost or out of place.

4. If you're going to be out late at night or in an area with a high crime rate, *don't wear anything that draws attention to you.*

5. *Project confidence and be aware of your surroundings.*

6. *Be assertive.* Sometimes even a smile or nod can disarm a potential assailant.

7. If you are a senior citizen in an unsafe neighborhood, it's best not to walk alone outside for any length of time, especially after leaving a bank or at night. If you must walk alone, bring a pair of dogs along—the type of dogs that can scare an attacker away, such as a German shepherd or Doberman pinscher.

PSYCHOLOGICAL GROUP AVOIDANCE EXERCISES

It is not uncommon for someone to be walking down the street and come face to face with danger. Groups of two or more people may be looking to harass, rob, or assault victims they can find on the street.

The following exercises help you develop skills to avoid such confrontations. Ideally, they should be practiced with two or more people. One person takes the role of the target while the others take the role of potential assailants. The idea is for the target to change the focus of the assailants. Also, when faced with a group of two or more people, never try to walk through them. Always go to the side. This makes it hard for them to grab you because they must go through their people first. The idea is to pass close to the street and not by the buildings unless the sidewalk is sufficiently large enough and the group is small enough.

Exercise One

As the group approaches the target, he looks them in the eye and smiles as he walks by. It's important not to show fear, so the target should not move quicker than normal pace.

Exercise Two

This time as the group approaches, the target looks across the street, waves his hand, and calls out, "Hey, Frank!" Of course, Frank is not there, but the group doesn't know who Frank is or if Frank is traveling with a group of friends. While a group may take on a single target, the problems that can occur if more people get involved may keep them from acting.

Exercise Three

As the group approaches this time, the target begins a loud, disgusting cough as he walks by them. Very few people want to deal with a sick individual who has a potentially communicable disease.

Exercise Four

While the group gets closer to the target, the target moves his head toward the nearest storefront or alley and sighs with amazement. He may even say "Wow!" This redirects the focus from him to an object or an area, and he is able to pass by the group without having a problem.

Exercise Five

The target approaches the group, and if he senses that the group may do him harm, he smiles and extends his hand for a handshake to the group member nearest the street. He can even say "Hi," as though he recognizes the person. This action does three things. First, it humanizes him in front of the group. Second, it shows that he is paying respect to a member of the group. And, third, it shows that he is not afraid of the group. As with any self-defense technique such as this, no method works 100 percent of the time, so always use your intuition when judging what action would be the most appropriate to take.

Exercise Six

This is a more advanced exercise to be practiced by couples or families. In this scenario, a family or couple is walking down the street when a gang appears. When they are within a yard or two of one another, the man places his hand on the back of his wife or girlfriend and gently directs her to the side of the street. If there are children involved, the woman gently steers them closer to the street than she is. A split second after the movement occurs, the man pretends to have an untied shoelace or an ankle problem and goes to one knee. The group's focus is shifted to him rather than on the wife and/or children. As the group comes closer, he stands up and uses one of the previous techniques, such as smiling, and then passes the group to the side closest to the street. This splits the focus of the group in several different ways, which allows the targets to walk by unharmed.

HOW TO USE YOUR ATTITUDE TO STOP AN ATTACK

I recently met a college student on a plane flight to Portland, Oregon. After brief introductions, we started talking about self-defense. She told me a chilling story about an incident that happened to her on her college campus.

One evening she was walking from the school library to her dorm room. Suddenly, a man started to walk beside her. He said that it was dark and that she shouldn't walk alone. She said no, that she didn't want him to walk with her, and continued walking. But he persisted and walked beside her, then suddenly grabbed her upper arm and began to escort her. She said nothing at this point. Noticing that he was walking slightly behind her as he held her arm, she turned around and saw that his pants were unzipped and he was behaving inappropriately. She quickly broke his hold and began to run. If it wasn't for her sheer stamina, she feels he would have caught her.

As we discussed the situation, I discovered that she never looked at her assailant—not once. When she told him no, she looked down. Her tone of voice lacked conviction, authority, and sufficient volume. When the stranger grabbed her upper arm, she didn't object because she didn't want to feel foolish.

In essence, she broke almost every rule of nonviolent self-defense. She was passive. She looked away from the assailant instead of looking at him. Her tone of voice signified that she lacked authority. She showed she didn't have the confidence or the intent or the commitment to resist. She was a perfect target and potential victim, and she was very fortunate to have not been assaulted.

An attacker does not want to pick a confident woman, because he attacks to demonstrate what he believes is power and control. Because such a man is insecure, he searches for a woman whose behavior and/or actions will satisfy his needs. Therefore, an attacker will not assault a woman who presents a possible challenge. He wants a sure bet. If you convince him you are not that woman, he will look elsewhere. Carrying yourself with utmost confidence reduces your chances of becoming his victim.

In his book *Being Safe,* Dr. Edward Ross urges people to keep their head up and eyes scanning the general area where they are walking. Be attentive and alert and never underestimate any potential situation. Ross notes a recent survey of state convicts who reported that they targeted people they knew would not struggle or people they thought would not chase them after they had stolen their purse or wallet. When asked how they picked their targets, one convict said, "I watched how they walked. If they seemed as though they have no energy and they looked out of shape, they were mine." All the convicts agreed that they were less likely to challenge someone who projected a sense of confidence and self-preservation.

The same principle is true for men as well as women. Your attacker is most likely going to be bigger, stronger, faster, and meaner than you, or else he doesn't have an advantage. There are some exceptions to this rule, and they usually involve drugs and alcohol. Sometimes a blast of liquid- or drug-induced courage can cause someone to think they can do more than they can.

There are a number of categories that represent attackers. One of the most popular categories is "the bully." If you think back to the people who were bullied in your school, what did they look and behave like? Why do you think they were picked on? If you were or are bullied, ask yourself "Why?" Then ask yourself what you did or could do to prevent this. Some people might say that those who were different in some way were picked on the most. The example often sighted is that of the obese child. But this may not be entirely true. Some obese children may not fight back, but others will. Consequently, it's not obesity that is the problem but rather an attitude of surrender. Chances are that the people being picked on were really nice people who didn't want any trouble; in other words, they projected an attitude that made them prime targets. Others who projected the intent that they would fight back probably never got picked on.

Bullies find their enjoyment in humiliating others. They are emotional vampires. Sometimes they travel in packs, as do wolves or wild dogs, and other times they travel alone. Either way, they seek someone who is not assertive, someone who won't cause them a lot of trouble. The more isolated a person is the better. The same behavior is sought for by the average criminal. They look for the easy score.

This brings me back to the formula for the commission of a crime. Crime = intent + opportunity. A criminal may have the intent to rob or hurt you, but without the opportunity he won't do it. Part of the opportunity is the attitude of the target. Will the target be an easy target? Part of this answer lies in how you look and carry yourself. The other part lies in your attitude.

Your attitude is the way you express yourself. It is your posture and your body language. It is how you appear to others. Consequently, your attitude plays a vital role in whether or not an attacker is going to choose you. Your body language is more powerful than the spoken word. It includes your walk, posture, eye contact, facial expressions, and overall appearance. How you feel about yourself and your surroundings is reflected in how you carry yourself. Your body language will tell others if you're strong and secure or anxious and uncertain.

A large part of your attitude in self-defense situations comes from your intent to defend your self. You have to make a mental commitment that you will fight back if you are attacked. In certain situations, this attitude is sufficient by itself to prevent an attack.

As for the bullies, you need to fight back from the beginning. This does not necessarily mean to fight back physically. Bullies work on trying to intimidate and humiliate you. When you resist them, you set up boundaries. And you don't have to be alone. In the case of school bullies or relatives or employees who bully you, complain. You can complain to other family members or the relevant authorities. If you feel threatened, complain to the police. If you are in a relationship with an abusive spouse, leave and get professional assistance. Either way, you are adopting an attitude of defending yourself.

Most of the time, it is this attitude that will warn a bully or criminal not to pick on you, since they both thrive on fear. The attitude of fighting back makes the bully evaluate the amount of trouble you are going to be. Even if the bully thinks he can beat you, he may not want to try if he thinks he'll get hurt in the process.

If you are walking alone and someone pulls up in a car and taunts you, and you fear that the problem will escalate, call the police, whether by using a cell phone or the nearest phone you can reach. If there aren't any stores around, say in a very loud voice, "I don't want any trouble." This will alert other pedestrians to take notice of what is going on, and it may make the bully stop the taunting.

If, however, you are alone at night, your options may be very limited. Make smart decisions if you live in a high crime area and minimize your nighttime activities.

Also, keep in mind that not all defensive measures work all the time. Sometimes when you have a bad feeling about a situation, you should trust it.

INTERPRETING DANGER SIGNALS

There are some concrete strategies that criminals use that we can identify in order to be safe. In *Humane Pressure Point Self-Defense,* the authors identify and condense seven signals that predict violence from Gavin de Becker's book *Gift of Fear.* They are:

1. *Forced teaming.* The assailant looks to create an attachment or partnership with the intended victim. The assailant wants to create an artificial sense of trust with the victim by being close to the victim.

2. *Charm and niceness.* These are tools the assailant may use to make the intended victim relax and let down her guard, because in our society we believe that someone who is polite and charming is a good person.

3. *Too many details.* In order to mislead an intended victim, an assailant will use "too many details" in conversation as to appear open and friendly. A skillful liar uses details to create the appearance of honesty and truth.

4. *Typecasting.* The assailant slightly insults the intended victim so that the victim feels compelled to disapprove of the accusation by cooperating with the assailant. An example would be the assailant saying, "You're probably too snobbish to talk to the likes of me."

5. *Loan sharking.* An assailant will do an unasked for favor, such as helping the victim with groceries, as a way of making the victim feel obligated or indebted in some way or to let down their guard.

6. *Unsolicited promise.* An assailant will make an unsolicited promise as a way to reassure the victim and quiet natural suspicions. An unsolicited promise in any setting is trying to convince you to do something he wants.

7. *Discounting the word no.* It is said of men that they take the word *no* not as the end of the discussion but as the beginning of a negotiation. If this is true of men in general, it is particularly true of assailants. This is a very important warning signal, and women would do well to learn to say the word *no* with forceful clarity. After all, many a would-be rapist has been schooled on the foul adage, "When a woman says *no,* she really means, maybe."

Another way of predicting violence is to look at patterns. If you're in a relationship and are treated badly, but your abuser keeps apologizing, leave and seek aid from friends, family, an abuse prevention organization, or the police. Continuous abuse is a pattern, and unless it is checked it will continue.

Other patterns that predict violence include threats—verbal or written—and stalking. If more than one negative action is taken against you, it's a pattern. The jealous ex-boyfriend who violates restraining orders and writes or says that he is going to kill may do just that. Take action at the first instance of potentially violent behavior. Action can mean calling the police, a counseling center, and even friends or relatives. Some people buy dogs. The advantage to having a dog is that they can sense danger before it happens, which may make them more efficient than a knife or gun, and, unlike a knife or gun, they can't be taken away from you and used against you. You can even buy a trained guard dog for further safety. The bottom line is that if you don't feel safe, you are not safe. Follow your intuition, verify the danger signals, and take immediate and appropriate action.

PUBLIC PLACES

Location can play an important role in the commission of a crime. Bars, in particular, have high rates of violence, especially for men when it comes to bar fights. Danger signals in bars are very important to recognize, because bars are often the playground of bullies. The bar bully needs a justification to attack, as do most bullies. Usually they stare at their victim to get a response, so they can say, "Hey, what are you looking at?" Other times they may deliberately bump you to obtain a justification to attack you. The way to beat the bar bully on the "Hey, what are you looking at?" technique is to do either one of two things. First, ignore him until such time as he comes to you. Then say very loudly with your hands up in the air, "I don't want any trouble!" This will attract the attention of the bartender, who plays an important part in this scenario, because the police usually ask the bartender what he or she saw.

Another technique is to get the bartender involved by purchasing a drink for the bully. That way, if an altercation occurs, the bartender can say that you purchased a drink for the bully, and then the bully went over and started trouble. This technique is for male-on-male intimidation only. As for the "bumping into" scenario, apologize and move away. Should the bully follow, put your hands out in front of him and yell, "I don't want to fight!" over and over while you take a step or two back. If no one interferes and you feel endangered, you may have to strike first. The impression on the patrons, though, is that you moved back, you didn't want to fight, and the bully ignored you. While this may act in your favor in a court case, it is always best to consult an attorney if it goes this far.

There is also a special consideration for females who are with a male friend, boyfriend, or husband, in a situation such as this. Do not interfere with the actions of your date or friend. If you tug at his arm or draw his attention from the bully, and if the bully is close to both of you, there is a very good chance that the bully will hit your date or friend at that moment. The best way to help is either to leave immediately to a safe place or to get the bartender or a bouncer involved quickly. When a male is engaged in a fight with his date present, his attention will be split between the fight and the safety of his date, which could mean disastrous results for him.

In fact, it's always a good idea to see where the nearest source of help can be located, and at the first instance of a danger signal, go get help. As always, follow your intuition.

HOW A WOMAN'S DEFENSIVE VOICE CAN STOP AN ATTACK

One should follow the principle that if one action doesn't work, you can fall back on another. Therefore, each new principle raises the bar slightly as it comes closer to potential physical violence. If one action doesn't work, you go to the next level and then to the next level, so that you have a number of options before resorting to physical violence. Following this principle of redundancy, the next component in your self-defense arsenal is defensive voice.

Defensive voice is a very important component when it comes to nonviolent self-defense. This technique works on a variety of levels. While many people think that it is just screaming, let me assure you that it has even more important uses and can be applied to many situations.

While many people may be familiar with the concept of verbal self-defense or verbal judo, defensive voice is much more simple and direct. Defensive voice is focused mostly on tone. It's how you say something. Both men and women can use defensive voice and may use it in different applications.

Simply put, defensive voice is a short sentence spoken in a commanding voice.

For instance, let's begin with dating. Whether you are dating or your daughter is dating, this technique may prove invaluable. If your date makes improper advances and you want him to stop, treat him as though he is a dog. By that, I mean you have to issue commands. Making elaborate explanations as to why you don't want to do something with your date may only challenge your date to overcome these defenses. It can become a competition that ends very badly for you. So keep your commands short, as you would if you were talking to a dog. You wouldn't tell a dog that you really feel they should stop what they are doing because it's inappropriate. Instead, you would shout "No!" or "Stop!" or "Go away!" Do the same thing with your date. Men are used to hearing commands and take them more seriously.

I use the word *command* because it signifies a specific tone of voice. If you demurely and softly say the word *no,* it will have no power. You have to use the appropriate voice for your commands. That's why, if you visualize that you're talking to a dog, you are more likely to get the correct tone.

Sometimes it may be a relative who is giving you trouble, for instance a "drunken uncle." You can use the same strategy. Being assertive and using defensive voice may help to control the situation.

Now let's move it up a notch. You meet a charming stranger, and he offers to help you with something, but the little voice in your head tells you there is something wrong. Don't say, "It's all right. I can manage." Instead, in your clear commanding voice, say "No!" or "Go away!" If necessary, swear at him. Some men won't regard you as serious until you do, although this may not be the same in other cultures.

This last scenario is often called the interview phase, because the assailant interviews the victim to see if she will fight back or not. If the stranger doesn't respond to your commands, you have a number of options left before a physical confrontation. One of these is to yell out "Stop!" or "Halt!" Again, feel free to swear.

Some martial artists believe that if you assume a "karate" stance while you do all this, it will be more effective. I tend to think that any attacker who has gone this far will see this more as a challenge to be dealt with rather than a deterrent.

There are still other options that you can use, and some of them blend the defensive voice with psychology. Depending on the situation, such as being stopped by a stranger, you can adopt a parental tone and say something such as, "I know your mother" or "You should be ashamed of yourself."

DEFENSIVE VOICE FOR MEN

A man's defensive voice can come in a few variations. First, there is the use of humor. For example, tell him, "I don't want any trouble. I have a bad back but a good attorney." Humor

tells the attacker that you may not be afraid of him. It may make the potential attacker think twice. While he's distracted, you can slowly walk away.

When faced with the potential for a fight, the target should raise his arms with palms out to the potential attacker and say in a loud clear voice, "I don't want any trouble!" Feel free to yell it out as well. This does two things. First, it sends the alert for help, if there are people nearby. Second, your posture and your voice continuously saying this may make the attacker self-conscious enough to stop his actions. Your physical posture may also make an attack less likely because the attacker may have a hard time getting an opening for a strike.

THE ATTACK PHASE

Whether you are a man or a woman, there are common strategies you can employ when attacked physically in public. First, notice if there are any people around. If so, identify one by what he or she is wearing and call to them for help. Specifically, you can say, "Hey, you in the red jacket and blue jeans, call the police" or "Help me now." People who have been selected in this manner may have a higher predisposition to call for help on your behalf, especially if there are other people around and they start to stare at the identified person. You don't have to stop at identifying just one person either.

Samantha, who worked at a check cashing business, had attended a DEFENSEWORKS seminar. One night, she was

followed to her residence by two masked men in a van. As she left her car, one of the masked men grabbed her arm. She quickly made a defensive move that she learned at the seminar and freed herself. She then noticed the other man with the gun. She quickly created distance and started calling for help. Her neighbors opened their windows to see what was going on. Some of them shouted, "We're calling the police!" At that point, the two masked men jumped in the van and sped off.

Samantha's tactics worked partially because there were people around. But what if you're all alone? As mentioned earlier in this chapter, there is the use of intuition and psychology. To this, add the commonsense advice of not going to high crime areas, especially at night. Avoidance is your best defense. Still, crime can occur when we least expect it. If one has discounted all the warning signs, forgotten to use the methods mentioned earlier in this chapter, and is physically attacked, the recourse with the most success, according to Edward N. Ross, Ph.D., is to fight back (see the next chapter).

ARMED ROBBERY

The response to someone holding a gun on you and asking for your money is quite simple. Give it to him. If you wish to minimize your losses, carry a drop wallet stuffed with one-dollar bills or play money as I mentioned at the beginning of this chapter. Depending on the situation, and if you are more than a few feet away from the criminal, you can throw the drop wallet in one direction and run away from the criminal. This maneuver doesn't guarantee that you won't be shot, but the greater the distance you create, the less the chance of becoming a fatality. Being in good physical shape really matters here.

In those situations where you comply and give the criminal your wallet, he may ask you to come with him. This is bad news, because the primary reason for this action is usually to hurt or kill you. Your only recourse here might be to try to run away. While physically fighting back is a possibility, unless you've had realistic training in gun disarming, it may not be your best option.

When Cindy was in high school, she was working in a pro shop on a golf course when a robber approached her. Frightened, she emptied the cash register for him. He then told her to go with him to the back room, where the safe was kept. He told her to open it, and she did. He then took the contents and left.

In this scenario, the robber was clearly only interested in the money. Cindy complied and was not hurt. Some businesses use safes with timers, or they post video cameras or post signs that the clerks do not know the combination to the safe. This, however, may not stop a criminal from reaching over to grab cash from the register. In retail establishments where only one person is working, hiring security personnel or the use of bulletproof glass and doors can be a lifesaver. The clerk, too, can use his intuition and call the police if he feels there might be some danger. Even if no explicit criminal activity has taken place, he can still request a squad car to come. It won't be with red lights and siren, but at least the clerk knows that help is on the way should there be any criminal activity.

If the retail establishment is in a high-crime area, the police should make a number of visits to it anyway, and the owner of the business should request it. The stronger the potential target is, the less desire there is to attack it. There are exceptions to this rule, such as when a criminal is under the influence of drugs or alcohol and doesn't have the reasoning capability to make this determination.

REDUCING ROAD RAGE

In today's society, the incidents of road rage are becoming more common. What makes road rage unique is that it often isn't done by professional criminals. Almost anyone can commit road rage given the sufficient amount of stressors in his or her life. Consequently, your response may need to take this into consideration.

The key to handling a road rage situation lies in knowing how road rage works and when you will be physically attacked. It is also important to consider that while we call outbursts of anger and violence "road rage," they can occur off the highway as well.

One of the biggest causes of violent behavior is stress.

Whether it's the stress from work or the stress from being fired from work or the stress from a school environment, some people internalize the stress and then blow up. One parent killing another parent over a child's hockey game is a good example.

While you cannot compel others to take some type of relaxation method to help deal with their stress, you can take one yourself. A number of people feel that prayer, Systema Russian martial art, massage, tai chi chuan, deep breathing exercises, acupuncture, acupressure, pilates, meditation, yoga, ballroom dancing, replacing coffee with green tea, surrounding yourself with positive friends, or even going for a walk can help to reduce stress. The key to obtaining success in these practices is to make them a part of your life routine.

What most of these disciplines have in common is deep breathing. Deep breathing can relax you and help you stay calm and focused. Breathing is simple. You can go to a quiet undisturbed place, sit down, and just breathe naturally. Listen to yourself breathe. The ability to relax can also help you deal with the stress of an attack.

Employers would be wise to offer some of these practices at work. Workplace violence costs U.S. employers about $36 billion per year, and stress is the biggest cause of violent behavior, whether it is the stress from being fired or from a domestic situation.

If you are confronted with someone coming at you in a rage and yelling at you, do not respond likewise. This is not the type of situation in which you use defensive voice. What you want to do in this situation, if you can't get away from the person, is to engage them in conversation and keep them talking. You should be calm, and your voice should be relaxed. Try to keep a distance between you and the other person, even if this means raising your hands as I mentioned previously, only this time use a low calming voice.

When you notice that the person's sentences are growing shorter or he's just using a word or two, this may indicate that he is about to strike. If you can, take a step or two back and try to keep him engaged in the conversation. Do not get angry, because this may give him the psychological reason he needs to strike at you. Stay calm and act as if you are trying to understand and help him.

Often these situations occur before you have time to take out a cell phone or summon help, so reassuring the person that you have his best interests at heart may be your ticket to avoiding a violent reaction.

TAKE ACTION

Everyone has a right to be safe. Unfortunately, in many areas of the country, personal safety is practically nonexistent. While politicians and pundits often make careers by blaring the "be tough on crime" mantra, they typically ignore the factors that cause crime to occur in the first place. Principally, crime thrives in areas of high poverty. There is a reason that a significant number of violent crimes with firearms are committed by young males under the age of twenty-one. Specifically, a sense of hopelessness permeates their environment and stems from a combination of poor educational opportunities, joblessness or jobs with low wages, and underpaid and overworked parents who can't spend the quantity and quality of time required to positively impact a child's life.

Picture a young man in this type of environment where his choice is to work (if work is available) at a low paying, dead-end job or deal drugs with the accompanying delusion of making quick money without suffering any negative consequences. For some young men, it is safer to live in jail than in their own neighborhoods. Consequently, the idea of spending time in jail is not a deterrent.

Another factor in the rise of crime is the lack of proper policing. Higher crime areas demand a higher level of police presence. In many cities, however, there is talk about using surveillance cameras rather than beefing up the police force, despite the fact that there's little evidence that this is effective. Great Britain, which has one of the highest concentrations of surveillance cameras, has not been able to stop terror attacks and reported violent crime has risen 12 percent between 2002–03 and 2003–04. The police officer remains as the best sentinel in the war on crime.

Being smart on crime means that citizens should request a higher police presence in higher crime areas. And there should be a concerted push by politicians and the business community to bring jobs that pay a livable family wage and provide affordable health care to those who live in higher crime areas.

ANGER

Being safe on the street has a new impediment. It is anger. More people are becoming victims of shootings due to anger. Anger is rapidly replacing drugs as the reason for violence. Falling mostly in the domain of young males, this type of violence comes from arguing, showing disrespect, and the poor choice of ego over common sense. While these incidents usually are trapped in the areas of lower income, the potential exists for it to spread to shopping malls and other areas of public commerce.

While we can look at societal issues for some causes to anger, we cannot ignore individual responsibility. Consequently, if you or someone you know has a short temper, look to ways of curbing it. In some cases, the culprit might even be hypertension or high blood pressure, which can be controlled through the appropriate medications.

Outburst of anger can also occur in individuals who are taking steroids. Often referred to as "Roid Rage," its effects can lead to disastrous results for the user and the people in his life.

SMART ON CRIME

The bottom line is that we're all in this together. If we ignore the plight of those less fortunate, sooner or later it will affect us all. Likewise, if we ignore the symptoms of violence in us or those we love, we will become affected by them. Stopping street violence means finding methods to prevent crime from occurring, such as working to reduce poverty, using treatment modalities for first-time minor drug offenders instead of incarceration, taking responsibility for our own actions, and becoming politically active and putting in place the appropriate policing response and set of laws for punishment as well as rehabilitation.

URGENT

Chapter
EIGHT

Preventing Sexual Violence

Knowledge + Action = Safety

Chapter **EIGHT**
Preventing Sexual Violence

"Those who are victorious plan effectively and change decisively. They are skilled in both planning and adapting and need not fear the result of a thousand battles for they win in advance, defeating those that have already lost."
SUN TZU, CHINESE WARRIOR-PHILOSOPHER, 100 B.C.

Sexual assault is a form of sexual violence, as is rape. Some of the best ways to prevent sexual violence lie in knowing who is likely to attack you, where you are likely to be attacked, what age groups are most vulnerable to assault, the time most attacks occur, whether weapons are used, and the type of actions that can halt an attack.

Statistics from the U.S. Bureau of Justice show that every 90 seconds someone is sexually assaulted in America.

- Approximately 66 percent of rape victims know their assailant.
- 48 percent are raped by a friend.

- 30 percent are raped by a stranger.

- 16 percent are raped by an intimate.

- 2 percent are raped by another relative.

- 4 percent are unknown.

In 2001, only 39 percent of rapes and sexual assaults were reported to law enforcement officials.

STATISTICAL BREAKDOWN BY AGE OF THE VICTIM

- Ages 12–34 are the years of the highest risk, with girls age 16–19 being four times more likely than the general population to be victims of rape, attempted rape, or sexual assault.

- 80 percent of victims are under the age of 30.

- 44 percent are under 18.

- 29 percent are age 12–17.

- 15 percent are under the age of 12.

STATISTICAL BREAKDOWN BY LOCATION

- About 4 out of 10 sexual assaults take place at the victim's home.

- About 2 out of 10 take place at the home of a friend, neighbor, or relative.

- About 1 in 10 takes place outside, away from home.

- About 1 in 12 takes place in a parking garage.

- More than half of all rape/sexual assault incidents were

reported by victims to have occurred within one mile of their home or at their home.

STATISTICAL BREAKDOWN BY TIME

- 43 percent of rapes occur between 6 p.m. and midnight.
- 24 percent occur between midnight and 6 a.m.
- 33 percent take place between 6 a.m. and 6 p.m.

USE OF WEAPONS REPORTED IN 2001 IN THE COMMISSION OF RAPE

- Only about 7 percent of rapes involved the use of a weapon (2 percent used a gun and 4 percent used a knife).
- 86 percent involved physical force only.
- 7 percent of victims were unsure whether a weapon was present or not.

While the Hollywood version of this crime typically depicts a stranger jumping out of the bushes, the sad fact is that most women are assaulted by someone they know as an acquaintance. But the acquaintance attacker follows the same formula for crime, which is criminal intent + opportunity = crime. This means that as soon as you feel uncomfortable with *anyone* (it doesn't matter who), speak up. Say no, use defensive voice, and if it is an authority figure, call a rape crisis center and/or the police. It is important to set your boundaries, be assertive, and fight back. If you are in an abusive relationship, leave. There are many counseling centers you can call to assist you as well as the police.

If you are uncomfortable about a situation at work, tell your employer. Depending on the size of the company, employers usually have a human resources department or an employee assistance program you can contact. If it's a small company, talk to the owner of the company. Under the legal doctrine of respondent superior, the employer has an obligation to provide you with a safe working environment.

In crimes of sexual violence, assailants act as most criminals do. Prior to an attack, most assailants check out their victims ahead of time. This means that the person you feel staring at you probably is. In addition to the danger signals I mentioned earlier, there are three steps that an attacker uses to check out a potential victim, especially a potential victim whom the attacker does not know.

Step 1: *The attacker checks for vulnerability.* Are you alone? What is the physical proximity? They pick someone to whom they have access. This may occur in both stranger and acquaintance situations.

Step 2: *Testing the target.* This is where the attacker takes a low commitment behavior from which they can easily back off to figure out what you are going to do. They want to get a feel for whether you are vulnerable or not, so they may approach you to see what you are going to do. Are you going to act passively to the overtures they are making? If so, that tells them you are the person they are after. However, if you act assertively and establish a boundary and call them on their boundary crashing, you are giving them a signal that this might be too difficult. In a majority of cases, the attacker will back off.

Step 3: *Locking on.* They have tested you, and you failed. So now they want to scare or intimidate you. At this point you still have your verbal and assertive strategy that you can use, such as defensive voice. This scenario may vary in the acquaintance situation, where the attacker wishes to cajole the victim more to get what he wants rather than act physically. Either way, tell them in a clear and commanding tone to stop what they are doing or to go away. Do not act afraid, as this is what they are after. Do not act indecisive, even though you may have a relationship with this person. The bottom line is for them to follow your commands. Have a cell phone handy and call the police if necessary.

Another option that people feel is viable prior to an actual struggle is running. But there are a number of potential problems with this action. First, remember that the person attacking you is usually going to be bigger than you are. So if you run, he may catch you. Second, if you are in a relationship with the person, the acquaintance may just call you over and grab you without giving you a chance to run. As always, assault is a crime of intent and opportunity. You may be on a bed or sofa or at a party and psychologically you don't want anyone to know what's going on because you are in a relationship with this person. You want them to stop what they are doing but you don't want to injure them. What can you do in these situations?

Obviously, the first thing is to avoid these situations. However, if you cannot avoid it, there are a number of things you can do. If you are attacked, fight back. More and more data demonstrates that fighting back is beneficial to stopping an attack. Also, running is not a bad idea, but you should first surmise if you can outrun your attacker. If not, then hurt your attacker first, so he can't run after you.

Most women have been conditioned from childhood to be passive or submissive and not to fight, so resisting an attack can be psychologically difficult. This may be especially true if the person attacking you is someone you know and trust as an acquaintance. Therefore, there are two ways you can fight back physically when all other techniques have failed. The first is to fight naturally, which means gouging, scratching, punching, biting, kicking, and just plain exploding on him. Focus on the vital points of the attacker, which are the eyes, ears, throat, and groin. The eyes can be most vulnerable when you can poke, jab, gouge, or scratch them. Make sure that you have intent and will follow through on your defenses and combine your attack with yelling or screaming.

As for the acquaintance assault, you can choose the same strategy, but oftentimes women hesitate to follow through because it's someone they know. If the person has not heeded your defensive voice and engages you physically, but you don't want to permanently injure them or can't call for help, grab their hand with yours and create a base by holding it against something, then with your other hand grab their smallest finger and pull it back toward the back of their own hand as you vibrate it. This will work on most people as long as they are not super flexible. If they are super flexible, concentrate on striking their eyes or scratching, biting, or kicking them as well as yelling and screaming. Always think: *I will survive.* Still, your best bet is obtaining self-defense training from a qualified instructor.

Carrie was barely 5' tall. A young mother, she had just put her baby daughter to bed when she heard a noise. She first tried to ignore and reason it away. After all, she lived in a very small town where crime rarely happened. Still, it nagged at the back of her mind.

She didn't have to wait long to discover what the noise was. With one thundering crash, her screen door hit the floor and a total stranger landed in her kitchen. No words were exchanged as the large man grabbed and threw her down. Carrie hit the ground and froze, not knowing what to do.

Just then her baby let out a cry. Although she had been petrified, the baby's cry turned her into a ferocious tiger. Her assailant was twice her size, but she fought back with a fury. She managed to get up from the floor. The attacker, obviously angered, picked her up as though she was a rag doll and threw her into the wall and then ran away. She recovered quickly and went to her baby.

Clearly, her attacker could have won the fight physically. He could have assaulted or killed her, and yet he chose to run away. When I first heard this story, it reinforced my belief that criminals want an easy prey. Once the prey begins to put up a struggle, there comes a point in the assailant's mind when his course of action just isn't worth pursuing. I call this "the flight point." The assailant makes a concrete decision to run away.

Additionally, according to Edward N. Ross, Ph.D., the author of *Being Safe,* major research findings on rape avoidance and survival show the following.

- Women can and do deter rape even in situations where resistance appears to be futile.

- Successful resistance can occur regardless of age, ethnicity, education, or lifestyle.

- Most types of resistance proved to be effective in some manner, such as calling a neighbor, making noises, or engaging in revolting behavior.

- Forceful resistance, using physical aggressiveness with or without a weapon, was more likely to provoke attack or injury, but those who resisted were less likely to be raped.

- The more strategies that were combined, such as physical aggression with screaming and yelling, the higher the likelihood of avoiding rape.

- Fleeing or attempting to flee was the most effective but least frequently used strategy.

- The most frequently used strategy—talking—was ineffective to deter a rape. Pleading was ineffective as it acknowledges the rapist's power and domination as well as the woman's submission, thereby increasing the determination to rape. Crying was also mostly unsuccessful.

- All women who did nothing to resist were raped.
- Women who acted immediately, aggressively, and vigorously were the most effective in resisting rape. Initially, aggressive victims were found to be twice as successful in warding off a rape as those who were not.
- Some of those who described feeling enraged toward their attackers for even thinking of raping them were able to avoid rape.
- In spite of offering no resistance at all, some victims were kicked, slapped, and punched as well as raped.

Nothing is 100 percent certain, but this knowledge combined with these principles may save a life. Although I have recommended mostly non-physical techniques, I always encourage taking self-defense courses. Every attack situation is unique. While fleeing or running can be effective, in an ever-increasingly obese society, it may not be an effective solution for long. Additionally, in some acquaintance or date rape scenarios, there might not be a place to run to if the assailant is already in the person's home.

Chapter
NINE

How to Deal With an Uncooperative Violent Felon

Refuse to Be Afraid

Chapter **NINE**
How to Deal With an Uncooperative Violent Felon

*"People should learn to see and avoid all danger.
Just as a wise man keeps away from mad dogs,
so one should not make friends with evil men."*
BUDDHA

P am ended up getting a divorce from her abusive husband, Gary, who ended up going to jail on felony charges. While some would say that his going to jail appeared to be a happy ending to what had been a horrible relationship, a significant problem occurred when the time to parole Gary drew near.

Gary was a chameleon. He played the model prisoner, but in fact he violated the law while in prison by contacting people who had a restraining order issued against him. This made Pam very concerned for her safety and the safety of her loved ones, because Gary threatened to kill her numerous times before he got locked up. She even believed that he could have people spy on her and report back to him.

What could Pam do to stay safe? In this particular case, they were dealing with a felon who was not being cooperative. However, his infractions of the law had not been reported because Pam had been unsure of what to do and was scared. Fear can cause one to withhold proper action from taking place.

In a situation where a dangerous person is about to come up for parole, there are a number of steps that can be taken.

PRERELEASE PHASE

The following actions may be taken to increase the chance of your safety while the felon is still in prison.

1. A letter detailing his violations can be sent to the Department of Corrections.

2. If a restraining order is issued against an ex-husband, the former wife may qualify for certain state-run victim assistance programs. Calling your state Attorney General's office or even your local state representative will get some answers.

3. Call the local or surrounding police department and join crime stoppers. They can provide additional information on staying safe, and in some cases they do a free security evaluation of your premises.

4. At anytime you feel that any state office is not cooperating sufficiently with you, give the governor's or the lieutenant governor's office a call.

5. If necessary, consider changing your name and social security number and relocating. This may sound drastic, but when faced with the possibility of death coupled with the lack of support from your state or from within your community, it may be the logical choice.

6. Take a reality-based self-defense course as soon as possible.

RELEASE PHASE

1. If the ex-husband is getting out soon and the political resources are not able to help sufficiently, send letters to the press making them aware of the situation. This may create enough pressure to keep the eye of law enforcement officials on him.

2. Obtain a certified guard dog or two to be kept in the house. This is one of the best defenses there is. Make sure that they are obtained from a certified and reputable institution. Professional guard dogs can be expensive, but so can purchasing and placing intruder alarms through the house, which is another option. However, if the dogs currently in residence know and like the felon, they will be of no use to the potential victim.

3. If the potential victim is still working for the same employer, make the employer aware of the situation. Also request that the hours of employment can be varied so as to prevent stalking.

4. Avoid going to the typical entertainment venues and hanging out at the same places, especially if those are the places that were frequented with the ex-husband.

5. Make your local police department aware of the circumstances.

6. Make crime stoppers aware of the circumstances.

7. Carry a cell phone, preferably one that can take pictures. Or carry a regular cell phone as well as a small camera. This helps establish evidence in case of a stalking or a violation of a restraining order.

8. Have the security guard at your workplace always escort you to your vehicle.

9. If you sense or believe you are at risk, call and go immediately to a shelter.

10. Attend a civilian police academy course, if the city offers one.

PROBATION

While Pam's situation dealt with someone about to be paroled, there are also measures that can be taken when an individual is on probation. Specifically, individuals on probation are assigned a probation officer, which is usually a state function. If the felon is uncooperative, his probation officer must be notified as well as the police.

Not all recommendations fit every situation. Rural areas do

not have as many resources as urban areas do. Consequently, moving out of a location may be the only choice some people have. The important thing is to take action. When a person announces that they are going to kill someone, they eventually will. Proper action must be taken and taken immediately.

URGENT

Chapter
TEN

The Importance of Intuition

Avoiding Danger Is the Best Defense

Chapter **TEN**
The Importance of Intuition

"Intuition is a spiritual faculty and does not explain,
but simply points the way."
RITA MAE BROWN

While the correct attitude plays an important role in conveying the "don't mess with me" attitude, we must always remember that most crime is an act of opportunity. This applies both to stranger attacks and acquaintance attacks. Even though the correct attitude may remove you from the target list in many cases, there is still the chance that the right opportunity may embolden an attacker to act. This is why we must exercise our intuition.

In his book *The Gift of Fear,* Gavin de Becker states that what intuition means is "to guard, to protect." Intuition by definition is a way that we can protect ourselves. Those feelings we have about something being wrong are generally right. In fact, de Becker puts forth the argument that we can even predict violent behavior.

The use of our intuition allows us to empower two other weapons in our nonviolent defense arsenal, which are awareness and avoidance. According to Chris Thomas and George Dillman, the authors of *Humane Pressure Point Self-Defense,* "Avoiding potential danger is more important than defending yourself if you are attacked—common sense is one of your best weapons. Stay out of circumstances where assaults are common. Be aware of your environment and of areas of potential danger. Pay attention to who is around you. If a person or a situation makes you feel uncomfortable, leave. Do not worry about being rude or impolite—trust your gut. Often your instinctive awareness of danger will warn you long before your thinking mind can recognize a problem."

While men feel that intuition is a domain mostly for women, they still recognize that it exists by calling it "gut feelings." So whether you are a man or a woman, you have the same ability to use intuition. Remember, if something feels wrong, it probably is. Intuition comes to us in many ways. Even dark humor can play a vital role as a life or death signal, such as getting a package and making a joke that it might be a bomb. Some victims of bomb attacks made jokes about the mysterious package they got before it blew up and hurt or killed them. Even saying something such as "I better open this in the next room before it goes off" is a vital indicator of exactly what might happen.

De Becker lists these messengers of intuition as:

- nagging feelings
- persistent thoughts
- humor
- wonder
- anxiety
- curiosity
- hunches
- gut feelings
- doubt
- hesitation
- suspicion
- apprehension
- fear

A simple way to identify what intuition is and how it works is to consider that you were born with two voices in your head. One voice is loud, sometimes shrill. It is an "I want it now," ego type, and logical voice. The other voice is a quiet, seldom heard, "do the right thing" voice. The challenge is to listen to the quieter voice of intuition.

For example, let's say you are a single mother waiting in line to buy movie tickets with your six-year-old daughter. A stranger says hello and makes an amusing comment about your daughter. Although he's handsome and charming, he gives you a bad feeling, so you step away from him. After the movie, you stick around and talk with a few friends. One of them offers you a ride to your car, because you parked a fair distance from the theater and it is now dark. The big voice tells you: "Don't be ridiculous. You don't see that guy anywhere around here, and it would be an imposition on your friend. Plus you would feel really stupid." Nevertheless, the little voice suggests: "Stay with your friend and take the car ride."

You decide to follow the big voice because you don't want to appear foolish. When you take your daughter outside the theater and begin walking to your car, the small voice suggests: "Go back and find your friend and get a ride to your car." But, again, you ignore it. Then, as you walk toward your car, out of the corner of your eye you think you see something, but the big logical voice says, "It's probably nothing—just your imagination."

As you keep walking, you see your car, but since it is late at night, there are no other cars around it. Now you start to get a funny feeling in your stomach, and you think to yourself that maybe the little voice was right. To assure yourself, you turn around. Out of the shadows the stranger whom you talked to appears. He's walking right toward you and your daughter. There is no one else around now. He's about thirty feet away and closing in. Your daughter senses something is wrong and asks, "Mommy, what's wrong?"

"Excuse me, but my car won't start!" the stranger calls out.

At this point you don't care if you look foolish or not. You grab your daughter, lift her into your arms, and begin to walk faster. As you take another look behind you, the stranger is keeping up.

"Hey, lady, I just want to talk!" he yells.

Your stomach begins to churn as you make a decision to run for it. Your daughter begins to cry. The car is now only a few feet away. You hear heavy footsteps closing in, but you're too scared to look back. You fumble for your keys.

Everything is happening so fast now, but it feels as though you're in slow motion. You have the car key in hand as you reach the car. Quickly you swing open the door and dive in, almost tossing your daughter into the passenger side seat. As the lock clicks the car doors shut, the stranger's body slams up against your door. He begins to strike the window with his palms as you start the car engine and floor the pedal. The tires squeal as you pull out of the parking stall.

Why didn't you listen to your intuition? Many of us have found ourselves in a scenario such as this but escaped. For others, the results are tragic.

When we understand how the big voice and little voice work, we can use them to more effectively protect ourselves.

INTUITION DEVELOPMENT EXERCISES

Some special units of the Russian special forces use a method of self-defense called Systema, or "The System," which contains various exercises to develop intuitive strength. To perform them well, a person must be relaxed.

Exercise One

One person stands with their eyes closed while another person tries to sneak up on them. The person must identify the direction that the other person is coming from by pointing at him. While this is best suited to be done in a park, any area that is sufficiently large will do. When doing this exercise indoors, it's good to pick a place where the floor doesn't squeak, as that will give away the direction a person is coming from.

Exercise Two

This is a more challenging variation of Exercise One. This time three to five people can be involved. One person stays in the middle while the others surround him on four corners, depending on how many players you have. If just three people are involved, then one person stands in the middle between the two others. With his eyes closed, the person in the middle has to detect who is coming toward him by pointing at them. Only one person should move at a time toward the person in the middle. If the person in the middle points his finger and makes a guess, he can open his eyes to see if he was right. Then the game begins over again. The players can switch places as they wish.

Should the player coming toward the person in the middle not be spotted while the person in the middle still has his eyes closed, the approaching player can tap the person in the middle on the shoulder if he gets that close.

Exercise Three

This is a far more advanced version of the previous exercise and should only be practiced if the players have done the other two exercises and feel comfortable enough to try this one. It is designed to create more stress while playing this game.

The scenario is the same as with Exercise Two, but this time the player has the option of running to the person in the middle. He can also brush his hand against their throat if the person in the middle hasn't made a selection in time. Once the person in the middle points to someone, whether correctly identifying the person or not, the session ends.

Exercise Four

This is a fun game called "Pickpocket." One person puts about a 6" X 2" piece of paper through their belt in the back. Then that person closes his eyes. The other person must snatch the piece of paper that's being held by the belt. The person with the piece of paper in the belt must have his eyes closed and can only stop the other person by sensing him. When he feels that the piece of paper may be snatched away, he can reach for it with his hand and protect it.

This is a great way to develop sensitivity about someone walking in back of you or trying to grab you from behind. Once you practice this enough, you will discover that if the person trying to snatch the paper looks at it long enough, you will be able to prevent him from getting it.

Exercise Five

This is a group version of the "Pickpocket." You should have at least five or six people to make this work, but ideally a group of at least 10 works the best. The more people you get for this the better.

One person is the observer. Everybody else has a 6" X 2" piece of paper sticking out of their belt in the back and is standing in a circle, which is outlined by a piece of rope on the ground. Parks usually make good areas for this exercise.

While everyone has their eyes closed, the observer goes into the group and taps the person who will be the pickpocket. When the observer shouts "Open," everybody in the group begins to walk around with their eyes open. It is up to the pickpocket to get as many pieces of paper as he can before he gets noticed. The people can prevent the pickpocket from taking their paper by putting their hand on their back to secure the paper, but they can't keep their hand there all the time—only when they sense the pickpocket is there.

Not only is this a good exercise for developing your sensing ability, but it's fun to play at parties, too. While it may seem strange that having fun is brought up in what should be a serious matter, the idea is that you learn a lot quicker and that you keep practicing those things that are fun doing. Also, by practicing with a spirit of fun involved, you diminish the stress and fear of an attack.

Exercise Six

Training your peripheral vision is another variation of being able to use your intuition. In this exercise, one person sits in a chair looking straight ahead. The other person comes from behind and starts to move his hand to the top or either side of the sitting person. When the sitting person feels the hand coming from behind or sees it in his peripheral vision, he says the direction the hand is coming from, such as right, left, or top.

Exercise Seven

This is an advanced version of the previous exercise. This time one person stands looking straight ahead while the other person uses a long stick, such as the end of a broom handle, to not only move by the three directions of the person's head but also between the person's legs. Once the person sensing the item knows the direction it's coming from, he can say left, right, top, or bottom. The idea is to first sense the item, but if that fails, to use their peripheral vision to see it. That way a person can build up a way to avoid danger before it strikes.

Chapter
ELEVEN

Martial Myths
Exposed

Make Sure It's Real Self-Defense

Chapter **ELEVEN**
Martial Myths Exposed

*"To understand combat, one must approach it
in a simple and direct manner."*
BRUCE LEE

S tudying martial arts has become very popular. Yet many
people engage in this pursuit under false pretenses. Not
every martial art is geared to be an effective self-defense. Many
focus on Olympic or tournament competition that involves
rules that are not practical to street applications.

While I can't go through every martial art system in the world,
I can expose a few myths about them. First of all, the term
"martial" means military. It should not be confused with the
fighting arts that are coming out of Asia. Almost every country
that has a military has a "martial" art—from ancient Egyptian
spear throwers and archers to modern Russian special forces.

I say "almost" because new countries, such as the United
States, grew up in a time where the prevailing martial art was

focused predominately on rifle, archery, and cannon skills rather than hand-to-hand combat. Older countries, for the most part, had indigenous hand-to-hand fighting arts. That may be the reason why boxing started to become a popular sport in America. While it was originally seen more as a modern-day "anything goes" brawling match, rules were introduced that tamed it down.

Have you ever wondered why boxers prior to the introduction of the Marquis of Queensbury rules always held their fists lower to protect their midsection? It's because the jaw is one of the strongest bones in the body, and when a fist strikes it, the wrist usually breaks. The Marquis of Queensbury rules introduced and mandated the wearing of gloves. That way the wrist would be protected, and the head became a viable target. Photographs taken after the rules were in place show boxers holding their hands up to protect their head.

This is also why many reality-based martial arts teach to hit hard with soft and soft with hard. Palm strikes are the most appropriate weapon for the head. Consequently, when you go to a martial arts studio and see people consistently practicing punching the jaw, realize that they are practicing a sport that has little self-defense application.

Sport martial arts, which are very popular with children, really have very little self-defense application. They rely primarily on cardiovascular ability in an arena that has rules so kids can learn discipline, and they match students up who are in the same weight, height, and skill category for the purpose of sparring and tournament fighting. The problem is that the person who attacks you on the street is probably going to be bigger, stronger, and faster than you, and he is not going to care about any rules of engagement. In fact, there may even be a group of people attacking you.

There are some instructors in sport martial art who may know real self-defense applications, but consumers who are looking for pure self-defense need to know how much self-defense is being taught in each class and how much is just taught for sport. If a person is looking to learn self-defense, the focus should be on learning an art that subdues larger individuals, protects against multiple assailants, and can teach how to defend against modern weapons, such as guns, knives, baseball bats, chairs, car jacking, and ground fighting. It should also teach how to protect your loved ones as well.

HOW TO FIND A REALISTIC SELF-DEFENSE INSTRUCTOR

In today's world, many sport martial art businesses advertise that they teach self-defense. This may not be entirely true. When sport martial art arrived on the scene around 1900 in Japan, its focus was to teach young people fitness and discipline. The idea was that once the participants were old enough and went into the military, they would learn the self-defense functions. In the military they would learn that in self-defense there really are no such things as blocks, but rather strikes that at times led to neck-snapping techniques. In other words, they would learn the techniques that young people were not supposed to know as it might injure them, such as pressure point application that leads to knockouts.

At the end of WWII, many GIs saw schools teaching the sport martial art and eagerly enrolled, bringing it back to the United States. Several Korean representatives who were taught Japanese karate, such as Shotokan, Shudokan, and Shito-ryu, brought this knowledge back with them to start tae kwon do in the 1940s, according to Robert E. Dohrenwend, Ph.D., in Volume One of *Classical Fighting Arts* magazine. He adds that "There can be no doubt about the deliberate intent on the part of both WTF and ITF Korean leaders to develop tae kwon do as a pure sport."

Other aspects that differentiate a sport martial art from a self-defense martial art deal with the use of weapons. While it looks really cool to be able to subdue someone who is wielding a sixteenth-century Japanese sword replica, it has little street use against modern-day assailants who use guns and knives. Likewise, training to defend yourself against one attacker at a time is of little help when confronted with a mass attack by a gang.

Proper self-defense training focuses on how to avoid getting into a fight, whether it is by developing intuition or the use of psychology. While many sport martial arts teach how to get out of a bear hug, very few of them teach how to stop a bear hug or a grab or a joint lock from occurring in the first place. Nor do they teach how to prevent a bar fight or how to take someone to the ground gently so as to avoid a much larger altercation.

Consequently, when evaluating and choosing a self-defense instructor, keep these commonsense criteria in mind:

- The instructor can provide you with verifiable information regarding their qualifications.

- After just a few lessons, a student should be confident and capable of effectively defending himself or herself from an unarmed one-on-one attack.

- The instructor can articulate the difference between sport martial art and self-defense.

- The self-defense methods that are taught are simple, easy to use, easy to learn, and can be done by people of all shapes, sizes, and abilities in a short period of time.

- The instructor doesn't try to convince you that his or her way of doing things is best.

- The instructor should not be secretive and tell students that they have to wait years to learn the answer to their questions or pay more money to become part of an "advanced" group.

- The curriculum taught makes sense to you and works on the street. If it doesn't make sense to you, it probably will not work on the street.

- The curriculum doesn't rely heavily on cardiovascular training so that only the most athletic or youngest can effectively make the martial art work.

- Realize that if an instructor is teaching methods or styles other than what they are qualified to teach under their certification, those methods may be incorrect.

- Instructors who teach choreographed movements, such as forms or "katas," should know how to apply those moves to self-defense situations. If you hear that the forms are done only as a mental discipline, then that instructor does not know the self-defense movements associated with that art. Originally, choreographed movements were taught with pressure point applications, otherwise a smaller person would not be able to subdue or control a larger one. If you are interested in studying an art that has natural movements and has been proven to work in modern combat and on the street, check out Systema Russian martial art at www.russianmartialart.com.

- Instructors who teach self-defense courses and focus on how to escape from a wrist grab are not teaching real self-defense. Men are not initially attacked by someone who grabs their wrists. Women are attacked that way only when their wrist is visible and accessible, such as when their hands are placed on a table or bar, and then usually by someone with whom they are in relationship.

- The instructor should teach the course without putting students in a big padded suit. The attacker on the street will not be in such a suit, and because it is psychologically easier to hit someone in a padded suit, this may cause the intended victim to freeze when confronted with an attacker who is not protected by padding. Similarly, when you are struck without padding, it helps keep you from tensing up and promotes a correct, relaxed, and appropriate defensive response.

- Realize that instructors who focus on demanding that students learn rituals, such as not pointing their feet at their instructor, focus little on real modern self-defense situations. You should also realize that while breaking boards may be a confidence booster, it has no street application. When confronted by a challenger who showed his board-breaking prowess in the movie *Enter the Dragon,* Bruce Lee said, "Boards don't fight back."

- Instructors who promote a self-defense course or seminar but are certified to only teach a sport martial art may use applications from the sport martial art that are not practical for the street.

Chapter
TWELVE

Terrorism, Travel, and Truth

Terrorists Win Only When Fear Reigns

Chapter **TWELVE**
Terrorism, Travel, and Truth

"In fighting and in everyday life you should be determined though calm. Meet the situation without tenseness yet not recklessly, your spirit settled yet unbiased. An elevated spirit is weak and a low spirit is weak. Do not let the enemy see your spirit."
MIYAMOTO MUSASHI

The bookstore was packed. My wife and I arrived early, but we could only find seats toward the back. Rick Steves, author, tour guide, and PBS luminary, secured the podium to talk about his latest travel projects and books. The crowd eagerly responded to his stories of adventures in Europe. After Steves' speech, the moderator opened the floor to questions. The flood of raised hands diminished slowly as question after question was answered in an insightful and amusing manner.

So what does this have to do with terrorism?

As what now must be the case throughout America, it would be nearly impossible for a discussion on foreign travel to no include some concern over terrorism. Finally, one person asked Steves about the chance of being a victim of a terrorist attack while traveling. His response was so accurate that I thought I would include it here. He noted that immediately after the September 11 attacks, many schools suspended trips to Europe for fear of becoming targets. Still, millions of Americans vacationed overseas without so much as a single incident of a terrorist attack. Meanwhile, three of the children who did not go to Europe as scheduled died in swimming accidents in the United States.

Rick Steves has been visiting and writing about Europe for decades. For those who wish to obtain his well researched advice as well as some smart travel products, I suggest you visit www.ricksteves.com.

You have a higher chance of being shot in the United States than becoming a victim of terrorists in Europe. As an American traveler, by far the most popular crime that you could succumb to is that of kidnapping. But kidnappers consider their actions primarily in business terms. If you are a successful business owner or a highly paid CEO, your chances of being kidnapped and held for ransom are higher than for the average vacationing tourist, but those chances are exceedingly low. Reports from 1999 show that the top five global kidnapping hot spots were Columbia, Mexico, Brazil, the Philippines, and Venezuela, in that order.

Obviously, if you work in a war zone your chances for being kidnapped or killed are greater than vacationing in a modern civilized country.

Fear sells, and the media is aware of that. A number of books are now coming out about what to do if you are kidnapped by terrorists. While their aim may be genuine, from a self-defense standpoint, the best thing to do is not to allow yourself to be kidnapped in the first place. This goes back to the principle of giving a robber your wallet only to hear his demand at gunpoint that you go with him to another location. If he has your wallet, the only reason he wants to move you into the alley or into his vehicle is to hurt and/or kill you. Why go? True, you could get shot and or killed where you are, but will it be any different if you go with the criminal?

Each situation involves a choice. It's best to make that choice when you have at least a sliver of a chance at survival, and the best choice you can make is to be as prepared as you can be, and not only from a personal protection standpoint but for your everyday life as well.

This also applies to dealing with the senseless acts of terrorists, especially as seen in the London bombings of 2005. Perhaps no country better illustrates the resolve to continue on with life than Great Britain. Bombed in the Blitz in WWII and by the Irish Republican Army (IRA), the British people have embodied a resoluteness to carry on with life no matter the dangers presented to them.

Terrorism thrives on fear. The more energy is spent on worrying about what happens next and how our travel patterns must change, the greater the victory to the terrorists. Obviously, one shouldn't travel when a sufficient warning about a possible attack is announced, but one shouldn't live in a constant fear of becoming a victim either.

So what are some ways in which terrorist acts may be thwarted? From Gavin de Becker's book *Fear Less: Real Truth About Risk, Safety, and Security in a Time of Terrorism,* come these suggestions regarding airplane flights:

- Limit bathroom use by pilots and eventually have bathrooms built within the cockpit space.

- Stop the in-flight meal service for pilots and, instead, stock the cockpit with preflight meals and drinks, because the meal service provides the most substantial advantage to hijackers.

- Fabricate and install cockpit doors that are bullet resistant.

- Install a locking system that makes the door's entry resistant.

- Install a system that allows officials on the ground to monitor the sounds in the cockpit if there is a loss of radio contact or the plane is off course.

- Have a video and audio system that allows pilots to observe and listen to the area outside the cockpit.

- Make cockpit security part of preflight instructions with words to the effect that protection of the cockpit door is the duty of both crew and passengers.

- Require pilots to keep cockpit doors closed at all times when there are passengers onboard.

- I would add that there should be increase security checks for pilots, cargo, and crew of private corporate airplanes.

De Becker contends there are also steps that you can do as a passenger:

- Pay attention to anything that triggers your intuition, such as two people who aren't traveling together but who seem to be communicating in some way, people who are adjusting items under their coats, people who seem uncommonly anxious, and people who are suspicious in ways that you can't even explain.

- Select athletic and capable people in the lounge or restaurant area and find out if they would intervene in the event of an onboard problem.

Terrorists, much like predators in nature, look for the easiest kill. Once airplanes beef up security, they move on to other forms of transportation, such as buses, ships, and trains. What can be done to keep these potential targets safe?

- Separate and bomb proof compartments for luggage.
- Create a separate transportation system to carry luggage only.

- Create smaller passenger train cars to limit a bomb blast.

- Use bomb sniffing dogs at travel stations.

- Run security checks on applicants for driving trucks that transport deadly cargo, including gasoline.

- Have resources available to check the cargo of ships at all our ports of entry.

Beyond this, de Becker offers sage advice in dealing with fear. "1. When you feel fear or any intuitive signal, listen. 2. When you don't feel fear, don't manufacture it. 3. If you find yourself creating worry, explore and discover why."

TERROR TACTICS

To search for an end to terrorist tactics is to study the history of such actions and their consequences. When the IRA embarked on a bombing campaign against the British in the twentieth century, it did not consider that a Unionist group, which formed to oppose the IRA, would also go on a bombing campaign against the IRA. As horrific as it sounds, these actions along with negotiations eventually led to a ceasefire and a workable peace.

While governments may state that they do not negotiate with terrorists, the truth of the matter is that they do. The Ronald Reagan "arms for hostage" scandal is one example. The issue lies in whether there is anything viable to negotiate on.

In America's battle with al Qaeda, there is a false belief that America is being attacked because of its culture. If this were true, then America would have been attacked since its birth, and the terrorists would have demanded that America change its culture. The terrorists of al Qaeda, however, have specific goals that deal more with the stewardship of Arabic lands than anything else, according to Michael Scheuers' book *Imperial Hubris*. Knowing this, wise politicians can apply the use of both the dove and the sword to ending this conflict, because terrorists win where fear reigns.

URGENT

Violence
and Spiritual Life

Try to Live Peacefully With Everyone

Chapter **THIRTEEN**
Violence and Spiritual Life

"He trains my hands for war, so that my arms can bend a bow of bronze."
KING DAVID, 2 SAMUEL 22:35

I s it ever acceptable for a person of religious faith to hurt someone, even in self-defense? Obviously, different faiths may offer different responses. As someone who was raised in the Judeo-Christian faith, I can best respond from that base of knowledge.

The Judeo-Christian faith relies on the pillars of the Old and New Testaments. Clearly, the Old Testament has no hesitation in allowing for the use of self-defense and in the sanctioning of violence and even war under certain conditions. It is where the doctrine "an eye for an eye" resides. But what does "an eye for an eye" really mean when taken in its historical context?

Looking back at the time the "eye for an eye" doctrine came in, it was actually a way to reduce violence and a step toward modern jurisprudence. While some people in today's society may find that practice repugnant, they fail to consider the circumstances that allowed the rise of this concept to prevail.

During those ancient times, tribal or Bedouin cultures allowed for the punishment of a crime to be conducted against family members of the guilty party. Oftentimes the punishment did not fit the crime. For example, a relative of a criminal could be killed for a crime that in reality did not call for so severe a punishment. This, as you can imagine, led to reprisals from the other tribe and an escalation of the violence.

"An eye for an eye, a tooth for a tooth" was an expression of retributive justice known as *lex talionis* ("law or retaliation") that may have originated in Near Eastern or Middle Eastern law. However, the oral law of Judaism states that this verse cannot be interpreted to mean exact physical retribution and goes on to state that the Bible calls for a sophisticated five-part form of compensation that consists of payments for damages, pain, medical expenses, incapacitation, and mental anguish.

What was revolutionary about the "eye for an eye" doctrine is that it called for punishment on the guilty party only, and a measured punishment at that. Therefore, it spared the relatives of the criminal and decreased the chance of tribal warfare. So under the rightful use of this doctrine, if someone steals a sheep and is caught, the sheep is returned to its rightful owner plus possibly another sheep or something close to its value is taken from the criminal and given to the victim.

This practice might have also helped in the capture of the guilty party as the relatives of the criminal would rather have the criminal face the consequences of his actions than any of them or their children.

But how can we square this with New Testament teachings that call for us to "turn the other cheek" when struck? Perhaps the best rationalization for this is that the Old Testament provides a foundation for the type of action necessary to distribute justice, enforce a code of behavior, and even raise an army to defend the tribe, while the New Testament focuses more on how to live to prevent violence from occurring in the first place. Although spiritual in nature, the New Testament offers the use of psychological tools to prevent violence and even fight injustice.

We can recognize two modern-day proponents in the use of nonviolence to achieve social justice in both Mahatma Gandhi and Dr. Martin Luther King Jr. While both men were killed, and some of their followers were killed as well, they nevertheless succeeded in their aims. More importantly, would they have even achieved their goals without using nonviolence? Can you imagine how many more people might have died if these men chose to use violence to achieve their goals?

Still, are we to die or to be hurt without resisting the violence in order to follow the New Testament? No, but we must look toward the entire focus of the New Testament. For example, consider the teaching about loving your enemy. If you love yourself sufficiently well, you will first seek to know why someone wants to become your enemy. Is there an action that you have done or not done that has garnered some type of negative feeling toward you? Or is it simply a case of a stranger wanting to rob you, humiliate you, or hurt you for no apparent reason other than ego satisfaction, anger, or jealousy? Consequently, is there a way in the New Testament to resolve these issues nonviolently, and if so, what type of preventive tool can be used in these situations?

Issues in which the parties know each other can best be settled without the presence of emotions, such as the desire to win at all costs, and in some cases with an impartial third party—hence the judicial system. This leaves situations where there is a potential for violence to occur and where violence is already occurring.

For instance, let's say that you are a male at a wedding party and are approached by a young man in his twenties who appears drunk, is loud and obnoxious. He's the type of person who is looking for a fight. Generally, two reactions can occur inside of you. The first is, "Look at that bum. Somebody should throw him out." The second is, "I wonder why he is acting this way."

These reactions can lead to two types of actions. The first is that you or someone feeling the same way approach this individual and tell him he's drunk, disruptive, and should leave immediately or face being thrown out. The second type of action is to approach this person with a smile, put a hand on his shoulder, and talk to him, inquiring what is wrong and engaging him in conversation about himself in a soft tone.

The results of the first type of action can be predicted when a shoving match that leads to a fight breaks out. Confronting potentially violent people leads to an increase in tension and the possibility of assault, especially when they are intoxicated.

The result of the second tactic is that the situation is resolved peacefully through understanding. Can you imagine how you might feel if a person approaches you smiling and unafraid. The defenses come down as does the desire to act out.

But what if this isn't what happens? Suppose the drunk was not coherent enough to understand what was going on and becomes violent. Are you then obliged to turn the other cheek as you get struck, under the New Testament? No. When Jesus says, "If someone strikes you on the right cheek, turn to him the other also," he means that the strike on the cheek is an insult and not an attack on your person (2 Corinthians 11:20). In the culture of the East at that time, slapping someone was considered to be the highest type of insult possible. So Jesus is really telling his disciples that they should have no problem enduring these types of insults. Jesus is not talking about a self-defense situation where one might endure physical harm.

In modern parlance, a good way to understand this is to say that when somebody insults you, don't insult him back or escalate the situation into a violent encounter. In other words, don't get mad when you're insulted. How many times have you heard the old saying, "Sticks and stones may break my bones but names shall never harm me"? Instead, walk away if you can, or if you can't, respond by saying, "I'm sorry you feel that way" and look for the first opportunity to leave.

So then, are Christians permitted to defend themselves and their families? The answer is yes as evidenced in Exodus 22:2; Numbers 1:2–3; Ecclesiastes 4:12; Luke 22:36; Acts 22:1; 25:10–11; and 2 Timothy 4:16.

The idea, however, behind the New Testament is to try to live peacefully with everyone—loving everyone as you would love yourself. That way, the existence of violence can be reduced and perhaps eliminated someday.

Till then, the best advice I've come across on how to get along with one another is from John Peterson in his book *Pushing Yourself to Power.* "No one should ever tell anyone else how to live, pray, train, or eat unless he or she is an example."

URGENT

DEFENSEWORKS
4947 N. Wildwood Ave.
Milwaukee, WI 53217

About
Wesley Manko

Speaker, Trainer, and Consultant

About
WESLEY MANKO

Mr. Manko is the Founder and President of DEFENSE-WORKS, a company specializing in conducting violence prevention, personal safety, and self-defense seminars and workshops to associations, corporations, and individuals.

He began studying martial arts in 1973. His journey has led him to obtain experience in police defensive tactics, aikido, tae kwon do, fencing, boxing, chin na, tai chi chuan, aiki-jitsu, Chinese kempo, ryukyu kempo, kyusho jitsu, combat hapki-do, and Systema Russian martial art.

In fact, he has been certified by Vladimir Vasiliev, the Cofounder, Director, and Chief Instructor for Systema Russian martial art and a 10-year veteran of the special operations unit of the SPETSNAZ (Russian special forces).

He combines this knowledge with an academic background that includes an Associate Degree in Police Science, a Bachelor's Degree in Criminal Justice, and a Master's Degree in Public Administration to produce a solid reality-based approach to speaking and training in self-defense. In other words, he only teaches the stuff that works.

Additionally, Mr. Manko has been published nationally in *Black Belt* magazine, *Self-Defense for Women* magazine, and @LAW, a publication for legal professionals. He has also been heard on the internationally broadcast radio program *Call in on Crime*.

On November 9, 2005, Mr. Manko received a citation from the Assembly of the State of Wisconsin for "providing a wide array of courses that have aided law enforcement, military, and civilian personnel including victims of domestic violence and sexual abuse in dealing with potentially life-threatening situations and preventing workplace violence through his public speaking and self-defense training that has benefited many businesses and organizations as well as his outstanding service to the community through providing lifesaving instruction in violence prevention and realistic self-defense training."

To schedule a seminar or purchase additional products, Mr. Manko can be reached through his website www.defenseworks.us or email at wes@defenseworks.us, or by calling 414-332-0599, or through the mail at:

DEFENSEWORKS
4947 N. Wildwood Ave.
Milwaukee, WI 53217

Unleash Your Greatness

AT BRONZE BOW PUBLISHING WE ARE COMMITTED

to helping you achieve your **ultimate potential**

in functional athletic strength, fitness, natural

muscular development, and all-around superb

health and youthfulness.

Our books, videos, newsletters, Web sites, and training seminars will bring you the very latest in scientifically validated information that has been carefully extracted and compiled from leading scientific, medical, health, nutritional, and fitness journals worldwide.
Our goal is to empower you! To arm you with the best possible knowledge in all facets of strength and personal development so that you can make the right choices that are appropriate for *you*.

Now, as always, **the difference between greatness and mediocrity** begins with a choice. It is said that knowledge is power. But that statement is a half truth. Knowledge is power only when it has been tested, proven, and applied to your life. At that point knowledge becomes wisdom, and in wisdom there truly is *power.* The power to help you choose wisely.

So join us as we bring you the finest in health-building information and natural strength-training strategies to help you reach your ultimate potential.